MW00490072

10 Top 10s

FROM A

10 Percenter

-

Over 100
Essential Acting Career Tips
From a Hollywood Agent

By

Brianna Ancel

Copyright © 2021 Brianna Ancel

All rights reserved. This book or parts thereof may not be reproduced in any form, stored in any retrieval system, or transmitted in any form by any means—electronic, mechanical, photocopy, recording, or otherwise—without prior written permission of the publisher, except as provided by United States of America copyright law. For permission requests, write to the publisher, at the address below.

ISBN: 978-1-7362981-0-7

ISBN: 978-1-7362981-1-4

Library of Congress Control Number: 2020925134

Edited by: Janet Torge

Cover Design: Beau Barcus

Published by Jordan Ancel International, LLC

Los Angeles, CA

www.tentoptensbook.com

First Printing: 2021

Published in the Unites States of America

Thank you...

to Jordan Ancel for your loving support & encouragement.

to Chip & Michela Barcus for your never-ending belief in me.

to Tim & Janeen O'Brien for providing an environment for me to thrive.

to Janet Torge for your way with words.

to Beau Barcus for your creative vision.

and to all my clients and colleagues, past & present, who have enriched my career and life with amazing experiences, friendships, learning opportunities, successes, challenges, and fun.

I am grateful.

"Becoming a working actor is one of the most challenging pursuits in the world. The competition is fierce, and many factors are outside of the actor's control. However, this insightful book demystifies those factors and outlines the necessary steps to break into the business successfully. Brianna Ancel is an outstanding agent who has helped guide my career for years. Through her informative book, '10 Top 10s from a 10 Percenter,' she can help guide yours as well."

- Richard Brooks, Actor
(Law & Order, Being Mary Jane, Bosch, Good Trouble)

"I have never seen a book for actors from the agent's perspective. Agents are an actor's partner in their 'business'. This has been a long time coming and well worth the investment in the future success of one's career."

- Sharon Bialy, Casting Director
(Breaking Bad, The Walking Dead, Barry, The Handmaid's Tale)

"Brianna is one of the Top 10 people in the business who really cares for her clients and advocates passionately for actors. You will learn a lot from her years of experience in the business and her insights in this new book."

- Anthony Meindl, Writer, Director, Actor
Founder of Anthony Meindl's Actor Workshop

"Actors, rejoice! This is the one book you need to navigate your Hollywood career. Top talent agent Brianna Ancel pulls back the curtain to reveal how successful actors mastermind their careers – and shows you exactly how you can do it yourself. Read it before you call your agent!"

- Adam Leipzig, CEO and Founder
MediaU

"Brianna is the most actor-friendly agent I know. What a rare and wonderful asset it is for an actor to have an agent who not only covers their back, but cares about every aspect of their business relationship – and that includes going the extra mile every time to ensure that a client's safety on set is the foundation for every job booked. I have enjoyed the gift of sharing a client with Brianna and her team for many years. I wish every agent I had to deal with had her experience, her passion, her commitment and her grace."
- Brad Lemack, Talent Manager *(Lemack & Company)* & Professor of Performing Arts *(Emerson College – Los Angeles Campus)*

"Brianna is among the most knowledgeable agents I've worked with. Every actor looking to find success in this business will benefit from this book. So much useful information in one place."
- Robert McGowan, Talent Manager, Co-Owner McGowan Rodriguez Management

"Brianna has spent her career nurturing her clients and seeing them grow into successful working actors. She gives her clients all her love and deep knowledge of the business. Not to mention how she's elevated Clear Talent Group into what it is today."
- Jeremy Gordon, CSA - Casting Director/Producer

"Well-respected agent, Brianna Ancel, has written a terrific book that every actor, or wannabe actor, should read from cover to cover. From soup to nuts, this guide will be invaluable to anyone who takes the craft seriously -- and who realizes that being an actor is as much about being a business person as it is about talent and craft. She takes you through it ever step of the way, 10 Top 10s from a Ten Percenter is a must-read!"
- Lisa Beach, Casting Director
(SCREAM 1-3, Wedding Crashers, Walk The Line, Logan)

"Brianna is a top-notch theatrical agent and a trusted resource who lets our company know what's happening in the agency world, its trends and what the agents need to do their jobs. Brianna's knowledge and ability to relay that knowledge is what makes 'Top 10s' an asset to any performer. It's a valued introduction guide and contains details every performer will continue to reference, as they further their career."

- Micheal Daly Director of Agency Relations
Casting Networks

"As a former aspiring actor back in the day, I truly longed for a book that would help me navigate making it in Hollywood, but I never did. Now as a talent manager and big fan of Brianna Ancel, I can confidently say, if you're looking to make it in Hollywood, this is the book, this is the person to listen to, and this is the advice you need."

- Johnny Webster, Talent Manager
Thruline Management

"I am so grateful to have Brianna on my team. She is more than just an agent. She is a friend, a mentor, and an amazing role model. Thank you Brianna for helping me to navigate my career properly."

- Brandee Evans, Actor
(Series Regular on P-Valley)

"Brianna is one of the best in the biz! She has a keen eye for talent and is an expert at molding and shaping the careers of her actors. Her knowledge and experience in the industry is second to none."

- Mike Page, Casting Director/Casting Executive

"Not only does Brianna have an incredible depth and breadth of knowledge concerning the ins and outs of this ever changing industry, she also possesses a beautifully generous well of empathy and understanding for humans and human behavior, which makes her an absolutely invaluable resource for actors. Her book is such a blessing for performers of all levels!"

- Andrea Bordeaux, Actor
(Series Regular on Run The World)

"A treasure trove of information! The definitive how-to book for actors. Brianna Ancel, one of the best in the business, lays it all out for you. This is essential reading for every performer, no matter what level you are at."

- Dan Shaner, Casting Director and
Assistant Professor of Theatre Practice in Acting
USC School of Dramatic Arts

"Brianna has an impressive ability to guide actors through whatever situation they encounter and she does it with kindness and grace. As an actor I have been through many ups and downs and she has never given up on me. Let her be your guide. She's a great agent and, more importantly, a good person. When she gives you advice, take it. She's got your back."

- Mark Gagliardi, Actor
(Series Regular on Blood & Treasure)

Table of Contents

Preface

As I was in the middle of editing this book, the world was hit with the COVID-19 pandemic. The entertainment industry was among the hardest hit, with Film, TV, live events, and theatre productions grinding to a halt. The necessity to social distance has created unforeseen challenges as creatives look to find solutions to re-open our industry. We have all been forced to find new ways to be pro-active, stay connected, and create art during this unprecedented time.

Throughout this book, you may find suggestions and tips which require activities and behaviors that continue to change as the pandemic evolves and dissolves. There are innovative and creative ways to accomplish everything in this book while social distancing. With any obstacle, we must all adapt as the situation changes. I know all my readers will use their own creativity and artistry to be proactive, even when the largest obstacles present themselves.

Please visit the book's website for addendums to each chapter as they relate to the pandemic:

www.tentoptensbook.com

Introduction

I wrote this book for you. I've been working in the entertainment industry as an agent for over 20 years. I know the challenges an artist feels because I feel them too. I am, in essence, an extension of the actors I represent. I share in their successes, their close calls, their setbacks, their frustrations, and sit beside them on their rollercoaster of a journey to create a successful acting career. I have also seen what works and doesn't work, and sadly seen very talented actors sabotage their careers due to complacency and lack of focus.

You've all heard: "Work hard on your craft at becoming the best actor you can be, and the rest will follow." But how many times have you seen a really amazing actor in a small-time theatre production or B-movie, and asked yourself, "How come that actor isn't working all the time? They're amazing!" The truth is: being the best actor you can be just isn't enough.

The actor's dilemma is clear: their passion also happens to be a very competitive and challenging career choice. To achieve success takes persistence, dedication, and a willingness to think like a businessperson— not just an artist.

Having an agent is a great start, but even that's not enough. We can only do so much. We have multiple clients and spend our days focusing on what an actor has hired us to do— procure opportunities and negotiate deals. I care about all my clients and want to see them achieve massive amounts of success. I wish I had the time to work one-on-one with each of them and micro-manage every detail of their personal acting business. But I don't. What I can offer are tips, action items, and steps an actor can take to feel in control of their career. I can help them move the needle towards achieving their goals.

Every item in this book comes from my 20+ years of experience: from working at talent agencies and representing actors; to observing and understanding my most successful clients as well as banking feedback and input from an extensive number of industry professionals.

Nobody teaches a class in this stuff, so actors are left to extract tidbits of insight from a variety of sources. I've put everything in one place for you. This book does not promise to make you a better actor— there are experts who can help you with that. Nor does it promise to make you a successful actor. It does promise to arm you with specific action items so you can feel in control of your career. It will help you establish practices and mindsets to make others want to work with you and it will provide tools to help you get the results you want.

It puts you in the driver's seat and helps you stay the course.

I intentionally formatted this book with numbered lists and bulleted items so you could read it one section at a time. You can open a random page and get a valuable tip, or even read it out of order and still get major insights. The most important thing is that you get what your career needs at any particular time.

Ideas and insights will be different for everyone. Some may need great strategies for staying grounded during their acting career, while others need to get their acting materials in tip top shape. Whether you are drawn to one chapter or another, I recommend reading them all eventually. You never know when you'll be reminded of a tool or tip you haven't considered in some time.

It can take up to six YES's for an actor to book a job, while just one NO can take them out of consideration:

- First, an agent has to say YES to representation.
- A casting director has to say YES to the audition.
- The producer has to say YES and sign off, followed by…
- A YES from the director
- A YES from the network, and
- A YES from the studio.

Six different parties determining the fate of what could be a couple lines of dialogue in a TV series or a lead in a feature film. Six different parties, most of whom the actor will never know or see during the process.

Well, I'm here to say YES to you.
YES, there are things you can do.
YES, you can build a strong foundation for your career.
YES, you deserve it.

And you're here because you're saying YES to yourself and committing to take proactive steps towards your dreams.

Embrace the journey that is yours and yours alone… **and have fun while you're at it!**

1 Top 10 Questions To Ask Before Making The Big Move

> ## 66
>
> I developed a sense of self before moving to crazy Hollywood, which was really important.
>
> JANE LEVY

Building an acting career probably means moving to the "big city" - a major life decision but also an exciting prospect. The entertainment industry glorifies Los Angeles and New York as meccas of opportunity for actors and performers. Whether it's glitzy Hollywood parties and celebrity sightings or the lights of Broadway in a city that never sleeps, they are both places where the allure of promise can make for unrealistic expectations.

As the song suggests, "If you can make it there, you can make it any where," which, translated, means: it ain't easy. There's much to consider when moving anywhere, but there are special considerations as they relate to an acting career. Ask these questions before making the big move and you'll be much happier about your decision... and more prepared.

Have I Ever Visited?

Imagine this – you quit your job, sold all your furniture, packed up everything you could fit into your car and drove to Los Angeles! It's romantic and exciting, the stuff movies are made of. However, after a month in LA, you are miserable.

You hate the traffic. It's more expensive than you thought. It's too spread out and you feel like you just don't fit in.

LA isn't for everyone. Same goes for NYC or any new and unfamiliar location. I've heard this story, more than a few times, from people who never visited the city before they made the move. They assumed they would love it so went ahead and made an impulsive decision.

If you can't decide between LA or NYC, spend some time in each. Take a couple months in the summer, feel each of them out and get your bearings to discover which one is the city for you. You have to enjoy where you live because you'll need a life outside of work.

Do I Know Anyone Who Lives There?

In a big city, full of millions of people, it's easy to feel alone, especially if you're leaving friends who would normally ground and support you. If you don't know anyone, consider participating in online actor forums where you can begin to network and make connections with other actors. On your first visit to the city, you might also audit some acting classes so when you do make the move, you can immediately join a class and begin to make some friends. Don't be afraid to tell people you're new to the city and would love to pick their brains for some survival tips. Having a support system is essential in the acting business so make a real effort to surround yourself with positive, like-minded people.

Which Part of Town Should I Live In?

As with any job, it's important to think about your commute. Being an actor is no different from any other work, except your job locations are casting offices and TV/film sets.

Finding a place to live that's centrally located will save you time, gas money, subway/taxi fare, and maybe a case of road rage. If those things are important to you, consider living near the center of the studio zones. Check out the SAG-AFTRA Studio Zones boundaries for what is considered "local" work in both cities. In LA, the center of the studio zone is the intersection of West Beverly Blvd. and North La Cienega Blvd. extending outward in a 30-mile radius. In New York City, the center of the studio zone is Columbus Circle and encompasses a 25-mile radius.

The distance of a commute may not be important to you. If you're moving to LA, you may care more about living close to the beach or Hollywood Hills; or you might prefer the affordability of places like North Hollywood or Burbank. In New York, your decision might be based on proximity to subway and train lines. Do you want to be near a park? The water? Broadway?

More than likely, you'll have many criteria when looking for your new digs. As long as you do your research and understand the lay of the new land, you'll be much happier when you finally choose your neighborhood. Yes, a happy actor is more likely to be a successful actor.

How Do I Get From Place to Place?

Subway or car? Cabs or buses? Bike? Uber? Whatever you decide, just make sure you're prepared to easily go from place to place. Auditions can come up last minute, or you might have more than one on any given day. Knowing the city's transportation options can be an important factor in deciding your move.

Yes, it's expensive to own a car and pay for gas and insurance. But it's almost essential in LA for a working actor. Expect to do a lot of driving. According to Cher's dad in the movie Clueless, "Everywhere in LA take twenty minutes." However, this is only true if twenty minutes really means an hour and a half in traffic. There are buses and a subway with limited routes, but both are too time-consuming for hopping from location to location.

In NYC, subways and cabs are the most common way to go. And expect to do a lot of walking. If you prefer to have a car, you should know it's going to cost you even more in the Big Apple than in LA.

5

What Time of Year Should I Make My Move?

This is an important consideration. Knowing the industry's "seasons" should inform your decision. If you give yourself some lead time and move when the industry is slow, you can get yourself settled and acclimated before focusing 100% on your career. Moving is a big step in itself. If you scramble to get settled while also trying to immerse yourself in the industry, you'll just add more anxiety to your life.

So, what are these seasons?

In general, the industry has two busy seasons: Pilot Season (approximately January through April) and Episodic Season (approximately July through November). These seasons are primarily dictated by the cycles of the television industry. Pilots are cast and shot in the spring (Pilot Season). By May, series pick-ups are announced in conjunction with advertiser Up-Fronts* [include definition in footnote - The upfronts are a series of presentations that the major TV networks produce each year, usually in New York, to showcase their fall and midseason lineups to advertisers, press, and competing networks with the aim of selling ad space].

Series productions customarily begin shooting in late July (Episodic Season) so that episodes can be completed in time for the fall premieres.

In the last several years, with the increase in cable and digital streaming programming, more pilots and series are cast and produced throughout the year and during the traditional "off seasons." But Episodic and Pilot seasons are still the busiest periods.

A note about film: although there's no definite busy season for film, there does seem to be a ramp-up to start filming in September/October in order to finish principal photography before the holidays. However, film casting occurs year-round.

It's best to make your move at least a couple months before Pilot or Episodic season. This will allow you time to get a feel for you new surroundings, make friends, and learn about your new city. You might even get a side job, secure an agent (who isn't totally swamped and pulling their hair out), and gear up to take the town by storm.

A note about weather: If you're considering New York as your new home, avoid moving in the winter. Weather in LA? Well, you know what they say: it's always sunny and 70 degrees.

Do I Have Any Savings?

Getting to a point where you can fully sustain your lifestyle on an actor's income can take time. In addition, there are a number of career-related expenses (classes, headshots, etc.) which are crucial to your success. Having a flexible "day job" or some freelance income lined up is important, but even more essential is reserving some savings to help you transition to the big city. Having a financial safety net allows you to take the time to find a flexible job and invest immediately in classes and workshops. Your savings can provide some security and comfort as you get accustomed to the lifestyle.

Making it as an actor takes commitment and perseverance. It's not uncommon for an aspiring actor to move to the city only to move back to their hometown because of financial hardship. If you have a passion for what you do, money shouldn't stand in the way. Plan ahead by starting a savings account prior to your move. Give yourself the gift of security and freedom so you can do whatever it takes to make it.

Do I Have a Part Time Job Lined Up?

The actor who is considered an "overnight success" is as rare as a winning lottery ticket. Most of the time, actors who seem to have instantly emerged as the next "it" girl or guy have actually put a lot of blood, sweat, and tears into their careers before that big break. It can take years before an actor makes a living solely on their income from acting. The reality is that you'll need to find another source of income while you nurture and build your acting career.

You'll want to find something flexible that can accommodate last-minute auditions and bookings. Be upfront, from the start, with your employer, stating that you are a working actor. Yes, use the word "working" so it will manifest as true, and so there's complete transparency when you need to ask for shift changes or time-off.

Here are some examples of jobs that allow schedule flexibility:

Uber/Lyft Driver
Postmates/DoorDash delivery

Teacher (acting or another area of expertise)
Web Designer
Restaurant Server/Bartender
Personal Trainer
Event Planner
Photographer
Office Temp
Script Reader
Massage Therapist
Fitness Instructor
Telemarketer
Substitute school teacher

Not a U.S. Citizen? What Are My Challenges?

I've represented a handful of actors over the years who initially didn't have working papers when I signed them. At best, I could submit them for projects being produced outside the U.S. But those opportunities were limited. In recent years, I've made it a policy that if I'm going to sign such an actor, I need to know they're in the process of obtaining a work visa or green card.

If you're considering moving from another country to try to make it in the U.S. entertainment market, your first step is researching how to obtain a U.S. work visa.

Your best bet is an O-1 Visa or "Extraordinary Ability Work Visa." Most production companies will require this form of documentation, although there are a few networks and studios that will accept nothing short of a Green Card/Permanent Residency. There is the rare occasion in which a network or studio will actually sponsor an actor for a specific project and obtain a work visa for the actor. However, it's not very common so you shouldn't wait around for that golden ticket.

You'll need to enlist the services of an immigration attorney to help you with the visa process. There's a whole slew of paperwork involved, including proving your extraordinary ability and why you would be an asset to the U.S. entertainment industry. An immigration attorney can help you navigate and complete all of these requirements. This process can take several months and cost thousands of dollars, so be prepared.

Doing your research and planning for this process before you move to America will prevent considerable frustration. It's tragic when an actor can't pursue their dream because they're unemployable due to their immigration status.

 For more information visit:
www.usimmigrationsupport.org/o1-work-visa.html

How Strong is My Brand? In other words, how do I compare?

Once you've moved to NYC or LA, you'll be among a huge pool – no, an ocean – of talent. This exciting, vast landscape of showbiz opportunity is crowded with actors, just like you, who want to make it. So, before you move, ask yourself: "How strong is my brand?"

In the business of acting, your "brand" is your Actor Identity (see chapter 4.2): the qualities and traits that make you unique. To assess how strong your brand is within the industry, answer these questions:

☆ What experience do you have? Do you have a lot of range and variety?

☆ What does your resume look like? Do you have mainstream credits? Will people recognize the work you've done?

☆ Do you have materials and assets such as headshots, demo reels, business cards, etc. on hand to sell/promote your brand?

☆ Do you have brand visibility? Social media, website, etc.?

☆ What existing relationships do you have? Are there people who know you and your brand who are in positions to help you?

It might seem strange to think about yourself in this context, as a brand or product, but it will help you understand the position you're in when entering the market. It can inform you of areas you need to bolster and improve to increase your marketability as an actor.

Keep in mind that, on average, your opportunities are usually proportional to the size of your resume. If you come to town with little experience or training, expect to spend most of the next few years in class, picking up small roles to build your resume and reel. However, if you're able to show some nice Guest Star, Co-Star, Supporting, and Lead credits from a smaller or regional market, you'll be diving into the ocean as a bigger fish and your opportunities will be greater.

Am I Emotionally Ready?

The emotional and psychological aspects of moving are different for everyone. Choosing an acting career means you've already decided to have a life filled with emotional ups and downs, which will constantly test your dedication, motivation, and love for what you do. Moving away from family and friends can also be tough. Add to that a new landscape filled with unpredictability, and your resolve and confidence may waiver.

You will need to remind yourself to persist, stay strong, and be patient. Learning how to completely focus on your goals can help you achieve both little and big victories along the way. These victories will be your fuel and will keep your batteries charged so when the hard times come alon g, you keep going with tenacious resilience.

2 Top 10 Tips For Getting Great Headshots

> **"**
>
> I've never taken a photograph of someone and created a persona. I've just discovered what was already there.
>
> ANTHONY FARRIMOND

Your headshot can be the single most important tool for your career. It can be the difference between a casting director glazing past you or choosing you from hundreds of other actors. Investing the time and energy into the best shots possible will maximize your opportunities!

Do Your Research

Choosing the right photographer is everything when it comes to getting great headshots. Recommendations from your agent, manager, or fellow actors is a great place to start, but it's important to do your own research as well.

You'll want to take a look at online portfolios to see if you like a photographer's shooting style. Check out their pricing and packages. But don't let the website alone be your deciding factor.

A photo shoot is an intimate experience between the photographer and his/her subject. Just because your friend got great shots from a particular photographer, doesn't mean you will. You need to feel comfortable and have a good rapport with the person taking your pictures. At minimum, have a phone conversation with any photographers you're considering. Here are some great questions to ask:

☆ Where do you shoot? Indoors vs. outdoors, natural light vs. studio lighting?

☆ Do you use an assistant or is it just the two of us? (If you think you may be uncomfortable alone with the photographer, ask if you can bring a friend.)

☆ Do you have a dressing room/changing area?

☆ Do you provide a make-up artist and/or hair stylist?

☆ How much time and how many pictures per look?

☆ What is your turn-around time for proofs after the session?

☆ Do you include retouching?

☆ Will I own all of the shots?

2

Choose the Photographer with Your Agent

I've seen it happen far too many times that an actor goes out on their own and chooses a photographer without consulting their agent or manager. Sadly, some have spent hundreds of dollars on a photographer they thought would do great work only to find out the shots were sub-par and their rep can't use any of them. Never think your rep is too busy to advise you about the right photographers. We would much prefer you spend your money wisely for a wonderful selection of headshots than prolong the process by having to shoot over and over again.

Discuss Looks with Your Agent Ahead of Time

If you have an agent/manager, get their opinion on which "looks" will cover your most targeted roles. Don't assume you are the best person to choose your looks. Your rep also knows the type of shots, wardrobe, and styling that are most effective and attention-getting. They are there to help market and sell you. Their input is crucial to ensure you get amazing pictures that capture the essence of who you are as an actor.

If you don't have a rep, talk to your acting coaches and teachers who understand the type of actor you are and can provide some professional advice.

Don't Get Carried Away with Looks

Throughout this book I talk a lot about actor identity and understanding your niche. You want to be sure your headshots reflect your unique range. Don't stray too far from the types of characters you are realistically going to portray. Anyone can put on a different costume, change their hair and make-up and transform into a totally different person. But you want photos that capture your sweet spot – roles that will most likely get you noticed.

The exception to this is commercial headshots because commercial casting is very look-based. Having a broader selection of headshots portraying vocational or "charactery" wardrobe looks can be useful and even required by some commercial agents. It's still important, however, to stay within your acting range despite the shirt on your back.

Find Examples

Just like when you go to the hair salon and show your stylist a picture of the haircut you'd like, it's also a great idea to find some images to show your photographer. Select photos that embody the attitude, vibe, look, and energy you like.

Sending these photos ahead of time will give the photographer an opportunity to determine if his/her location and lighting can capture what you want. It also prepares them for what's expected and can help you get better headshots.

But be careful! Make sure you're still "you" in the pictures. Your unique look and feel needs to come through. Don't try to mimic or copy someone else's headshot exactly. Example photos can be wonderful for inspiration and as a guide, but once you're in front of the camera, let your own light shine!

Ladies, Less is More. Men, Some is More.

By this, I mean Make-Up (I know what all your dirty minds were thinking!). Make-up is a very important part of your photo shoot. Without it, headshots can look unprofessional and you'll end up spending a lot of money retouching where make-up on the shoot could have helped.

However, keeping your make-up natural with just a touch of color is going to yield far better photos than a full face of stage make-up. Heavy eye shadows, eye liners, dark lipsticks and overly blushed cheeks are usually too extreme for a basic headshot.

To all my clients, I recommend hiring a make-up artist... it's totally worth it. A good make-up artist will know exactly how much to apply so that your features are accentuated without overly glamourizing your face.

There is a time and place, however, to have more freedom with or without make-up in a headshot. To capture a specific look, you might need bright red lips (period/retro), a heavy, dark eye (edgy/goth) or no make-up at all (victim/life-worn/homeless). You get the idea. Just make sure your primary headshots look like the person who's going to walk into the audition room.

For guys, you might not think you need any make-up, but consider a photo shoot like being on a film set. Bright lights bring out every flaw, so some light powder or concealer for problem areas can make all the difference. You may not need to hire a make-up artist but having your own make-up on hand that matches your skin tone is useful for more than just a photo shoot. So, men: some make-up can definitely enhance your photos... and your chances.

Be an Actor in Your Headshots, Not a Model

Getting a great headshot is only half the responsibility of the photographer. As the subject, it is equally important that you give the photographer some great moments to capture. For some people, getting headshots taken is worse than going to the dentist. It's not uncommon to feel stiff, phony, shy or self-conscious. My best advice is to stop trying to model and pose and just be the actor that you are! Models pose, actors act.

As you have your photos taken, live within the characters that represent each headshot look. What would they be thinking? How would they look at people? Apply what you've learned in your acting classes to your photo shoot. It may seem challenging since you have to be still, but when you let the actor in you out, you will have more fun with the shoot. Relax, perform, and you'll get amazing pictures.

Trust Your Agent's Selects

You've had your headshots session, now comes the very important process of selecting which shots to use. Everyone has an opinion and all opinions are valid. However, you must understand that your agent/ manager is an expert in marketing and selling actors. They know which pictures work and which don't. They can see the ones that will catch the eye of casting directors in a pool of hundreds of other actors. When your agent selects your headshot photos, trust they've chosen shots they feel will get you in the door. If there are pictures you absolutely love which they don't select, put them on your website, social media or press material. You can show them off that way.

Retouching - Keep it Real

There's nothing worse than an overly retouched headshot... well, maybe

I can think of a few things worse. But in the land of actor photos, a shot that has been photoshopped to death, will literally kill your chances of getting in the room. Casting directors want to see the same person walk in the room they selected from the headshot. If your picture is so retouched that every tiny wrinkle is gone and you look 15 years younger than in person, it's not going to go over too well in the casting room.

Subtle wrinkle retouching is fine, but make sure you keep the character of your face. Retouching should be limited to fixing blemishes, temporary skin flaws, fly-away hairs, smoothing some wrinkles, adjusting shadows, removing dark under-eyes, color correction, and lighting adjustments. Avoid making the whites of your eyes whiter (this rarely looks real), over--smoothing, removing moles and freckles and adding any contouring. What you don't want is an airbrushed look which takes away any dimension in your face and makes you look flat. The goal of headshot retouching is to look like your picture was never retouched. Aging is a reality and it can be the reason you were called in for a particular role, so live up to the look and you're more likely to be booked. Be true to you.

Remember the Goal

The goal of your headshot session is very simple – to capture who you are as an actor in the most authentic and eye-catching way. All the tips above will help you achieve great shots, but if you forget the goal, you'll end up with pictures you aren't satisfied with.

This is not the time to play America's Next Top Model. It's not the time to try to become another actor, nor is it time to be lackluster or uncommitted to the goal at hand. This is a hugely important investment in your career and one that you'll make multiple times. You owe it to yourself and your reps to consider it as such. Put thought into it, do your homework, prepare, and have fun. Embody your actor identity in your photos and you'll get the "money shots".

3 Top 10 Tips For A Great Resume & Demo Reel

> ❝
>
> You have to remind casting directors out here that you don't just do one thing. There's a lot of people who do just one thing.

STEPHEN ROOT

In sales, how you present your product can make or break whether a customer makes a purchase. The same goes for your acting career. Aside from the all-important headshot, your resumé and demo reel are equally important. This trio of materials is your calling card. They are often the only things you or your agent have to win one of those precious audition slots. Below are some essential tips for getting your resumé, demo reel, and electronic press kit (EPK) in top shape so you can stand out from the rest.

Quality Over Quantity

RESUMÉ: For up and coming actors, it's tempting to list anything and everything you've ever done on your resumé. Being discerning when it comes to credits can be one of the hardest things to do because it means editing out some of your work. But in the long run, a resumé that contains quality over quantity will give you greater credibility as a top working actor. Consider eliminating background extra work, jobs in which your part got cut or roles for which you don't have any footage to show. As your resumé grows, you may also phase out credits which have become less important to your career.

DEMO: The same goes for your demo reel. Including poor-quality scenes which don't show you in the best light (literally and figuratively) can have a detrimental effect on how people see you as an actor. All actors have been a part of a project that wasn't so great: bad sound, poor direction, subpar supporting actors. Many factors can contribute to disappointing footage. Unfortunately, that footage can also make your strong performance appear weak.

You're better off waiting to create a demo when you have a few things of decent quality, of which you are proud and can serve as an appropriate video resumé of your work.

RESUMÉ: Include Directors

This may seem obvious, but I've seen too many resumes without the project directors listed. Whether a film or television show, listing the director adds another point of reference for anyone examining your resumé. They may not have heard of the project but have heard of the director. Who you've worked with can tell someone a lot about your style of acting. For instance, if you've worked with Aaron Sorkin, this tells us you've been able to adapt to his rapid-fire, overlapping dialogue style.

The standard method is to list the directors as follows: in the third column, "production company or network / director".

In the world of commercial acting, it's not customary to list the commercials in which you've appeared on your resumé – it can cause product conflicts for new work. But listing the directors you've worked with in various commercials is a great alternative and adds credibility.

Joan Doe

SAG-AFTRA, AEA (*or other union status's*)

Height: 5'6" Weight: 134 lbs. Eyes: Brown Hair: Brown (for now)

Agency and/or Manager logo can go here

TV

Hunters	Recurring Guest Star	Amazon / Various
Blue Bloods	Guest Star	CBS / Rachel Feldman
Henry Danger	Co-Star	Nickelodeon / Ron Mena
The Affair	Co-Star	Showtime / Josh Jackson
Jane the Virgin	Co-Star	CW / Gina Rodriguez
Doubt	Co-Star	CBS / Daisy Mayer

FILM

Female Fight Squad*	Supporting/Stunts	Cineville / Miguel Ferrer
Me Him Her	Supporting	FilmBuff / Max Landis
A Place We Go To	Lead	New Marching Films / Jenny Wang
Tomorrow	Supporting	Futurescope Films / Martha Pinson

*Winner, Audience Award, 2020 Small Town Film Festival

THEATER

The Three Sisters	Natalie	Int'l Fest. of Arts & Ideas/Dmitry Krymov
Owners	Mary u/s	Yale Repertory Theatre/ Evan Yionoulis
Staging Wittgenstein	Defective Person	Edinburgh Fringe Festival / Blair Simmons
Oliver	Charlene	Berkeley Playhouse Theatre
Ebenezer	Ensemble	Windermere Middle School

INTERNET/NEW MEDIA

Release	Co-Star	Topic Studios / Ryan Morrison
Solve	Recurring	SnapChat / John Cvak
Nina Unlocked	Series Regular	Recursor.tv / Martin Hall

COMMERCIALS

List available upon request. Directors worked with: Johnny Miller, Cara Cristo, Brit Mason, Oliver Jones

TRAINING

UCLA, School of Acting, B.F.A.

Scene Study: Larry Moss, Karl Bury, Polina Klimovitskaya, Stuart Burney.

Shakespeare: Patsy Rodenburg, British American Drama Academy (BADA).

On-Camera: Bob Krakower, Ted Sluberski, Kelly Kimball, Peter Miner, Ellen Novack.

Comedy/Improvisation: Upright Citizens Brigade (UCB).

SPECIAL SKILLS

Fluent Spanish, Jazz singer (soprano), Dance (Tap, Ballet, Hip-Hop), Guitar (10+ years), Triathlon, Motorcycle License, Valid U.S. Passport, Experienced Black-Jack Dealer, Certified Yoga Instructor,

CONTACT: (*include agent and/or manager, or your phone number and email address*)

3

RESUMÉ: Don't Over-Embellish

I'm pretty sure there's not a resume I've seen that hasn't taken some liberties in describing a particular credit. Everyone does it. However, there are some embellishments you should steer clear of because they can be easily fact-checked and backfire on you.

◊ Indicating you were credited when you were really an Extra. If you worked as an Extra, IMDB will show you as uncredited, which in most instances is a sign that you were a background extra on a project. There's nothing wrong with this, but make sure you list it properly. You can put the name of the Extras group (ie: "Crowd Member") or simply "Background." I suggest you only include background credits on a resumé if you have little else to show.

◊ TV Credits. When you're hired for a television show, it's made very clear upfront how you will be billed (Under Five, Co-Star, Guest Star, Series Regular), so it's best not to fudge this on a resumé. A casting director might catch you in a lie if they see a credit for a show they've cast and realize: "Hey, we never booked them as a Guest Star." Or, when your agent is asked for a Guest Star quote because your resumé has a Guest Star credits. If it's not true, it can mean an embarrassing encounter with casting and mistrust between you and your agent. If you're unsure about how to list something, discuss it with your rep.

◊ "Uncle Jerry's School of Acting." Don't make stuff up just to fill up your resume. Even if you think: "No one will ever take the time to prove I didn't go to this acting school"… it's just not worth it.

◊ Be honest. It's better to provide a true picture of where you are in your career than to pad a resumé with BS. We're trained professionals and can sniff it out.

RESUMÉ: Be Specific in Your Special Skills

Expert Horseback Rider? Championship Salsa Dancer? Baton Twirler? For any performer, resumé credits don't tell the whole story and range of one's skills. The Special Skills section of your resumé is the place to brag about your many talents. Keep them interesting and make sure they're special and noteworthy. Consider only skills in which you excel beyond average and those which could be an asset to a particular project.

Aside from performing arts-related skills (singing, dancing, instruments, etc.), here are some other beneficial skills to include:

◊ Fluent Languages / Dialects

◊ Certifications (i.e. CPR, Pilates, EMT, personal trainer)

◊ Actual Military Experience

◊ Citizenship (particularly dual with another country)

◊ Multiple Passport Holder

◊ Sports Accomplishments (i.e. All-State, National Champion)

◊ Celebrity Impressions (list)

◊ Martial Arts and/or Stunts

◊ Weapons Training

◊ Advanced Vocational Skills (i.e. firefighter, yoga instructor, mixologist, DJ, lawyer)

◊ Special Driving Licenses (i.e. motorcycle, big rig, pilot)

◊ Teleprompter Experience

I'm also a big fan of throwing in a couple of random & fun skills that make for good conversation starters. I've had clients include things like: Air Guitar Champion (true story), crocheting jar covers (was on a male actor's special skills), can say the alphabet backwards, and able to solve a Rubik's cube. Have fun with it and give us a peek into your personality!

RESUMÉ: Do <u>Not</u> Include Your Address; Do Include Your Contact Info

Let's face it, there are some questionable individuals in the acting world. Data privacy is becoming more and more important and you should always be conscientious about what personal information you give freely.

On a traditional employment resumé it's common to include a home address but in the entertainment industry it's not expected. It's scary to think your headshot and resumé could get into the hands of a nefarious person who would then also know where you live.

The only personal info you should include is your phone number and your email address. Or, if you have an agent or manager, replace yours with theirs. Your email should be simple and professional, preferably your name@ or a form of your name. Avoid cheeky emails like "risingstar123@", "superstar007@", or "everydayimhustlin@". They don't sound professional. If needed, create a new email address for your acting career and business.

Be sure your voicemail has a professional message. A producer friend of mine said he actually did not hire someone because, when he called, he got a lame and immature voicemail. Never let your voicemail get so full that no one can leave you a message. What if that was THE call you've been waiting for? Better yet, if you have an agent or manager, you should replace your phone/email with those of your reps.

DEMO REEL: No Montages

Just get to the point. There used to be a popular trend of creating a montage introduction at the start of an actor's demo reel, with quick moments from their body of work, edited together in a flashy sizzle reel with a music track over the top. While I understand the temptation – "look at my range, character types, and emotional states"– what really matters is the substance of the scenes. A title card at the front of your demo with your name and contact info (and/or rep's) is all that's needed. And then just get into it. If you can't help yourself, put the montage at the end, as a sort of "in summary" closer.

There is a huge lack of patience in this business. The goal is for the industry professional watching your demo to see the meat of your work right away. Believe it or not, skimming off 20 seconds of fluff can make a big difference. Use those first 20 seconds to grab them with a great scene. Otherwise they may hit stop before you've even started.

DEMO REEL: Include Titles

This is a personal preference, and I know that many agents and managers are partial to it as well. The idea is to let your audience know what they're watching. We could probably figure out the film or TV show by the actors you're with or by the network logo on the screen. But make it easy and just tell us. This is most important for independently produced work which is less recognizable. Having the title briefly superimposed at the beginning of the scene also helps connect the scene to your resumé credit.

DEMO REEL: Choose Your Scenes Wisely & Keep It Moving

To make the biggest impact, be thoughtful about the scenes you choose and the length of your demo.

Similar to how you craft your resumé, it's important to be selective: you don't need to include every clip of acting work you've accumulated. If you were a painter, holding a gallery showing, would you present every painting you ever completed? Probably not. You would choose your best pieces so people could see your true talent. Every actor has work they aren't entirely proud of. It's part of the journey. But, in a demo reel, you can be in control of what people see. I've seen more demos crash and burn because the actor chose to include work from projects that are just flat-out bad. This does nothing to help an actor's career. I would rather see two strong scenes, over five scenes of bad quality, bad direction and bad acting.

Try to keep the length to 3-5 minutes max of substantial content. If you have a huge body of work, you might stretch this, but no more than 6 minutes is advised. The goal of your demo should be to keep the viewer engaged so they want to watch the entire reel.

The order of your scenes should be chosen wisely. Typically, you should start with your strongest or most recent content. If those scenes are from a project which is not very recognizable, then consider starting with a scene that may be smaller, but more familiar. You want to establish credibility and show that you've booked mainstream projects.

When possible, mix up the variety of characters to show your range. For example, if you have 3 scenes playing law enforcement, avoid grouping them consecutively. Choose an order that provides contrast so your range as an actor is revealed and you aren't pigeonholed into a particular type of character.

And lastly, if you have a large body of both dramatic and comedic work, it's a good idea to create two demos– one for drama and one for comedy. I have several clients with both and it's helpful to have a dedicated reel when creating a targeted pitch for a specific genre.

As you play with the length and the order, get opinions from your agent, manager and community until you've fine-tuned your demo into a work of art!

DEMO REEL: Make It Downloadable

The most convenient way to share your materials is through a downloadable link. Demo reels and photo files can be huge and we all hate getting massively large attachments in our Inbox. Sending files in this manner is a sure way to irritate the intended recipient and often, a large message may not even reach them. When a casting director requests an actor's demo, they typically want it to be downloadable, so you'll be ahead of the game.

My personal preference for demo reels is Vimeo.com. By hosting your reel on Vimeo, you'll get the added perk of having the option to track analytics, such as the number of views and number of downloads. Vimeo can even tell you if people are watching your videos until the end or at what point they're checking out. This can be valuable information and might motivate you to rethink the order of your reel.

If you do send attachments, I recommend attaching only compressed versions of your resumé and headshots (less than 1 MB total). Include your demo reel and all your materials in one downloadable link. Or, better yet, host all your materials on your website!

Electronic Press Kit (EPK)

An EPK is a digital collection of all your materials and can be a tremendously useful marketing tool. EPK's are presented in a visually eye-catching way (usually a PDF file) in order to promote and sell yourself to agents, managers, casting directors, producers, ad agencies, press outlets, etc. EPKs have been used by the music industry and publicists for years but are now commonly used by actors.

An actor's EPK should include all or some of the following: resumé highlights, press clippings, interviews, photo stills from projects you've worked on, tear sheets from modeling gigs, links to online content/ demos, discography (for recording artists), bio, performance reviews, website, social media handles, charity/philanthropic involvement and your representatives and their contact info. Think of it as a collage or bulletin board of all your assets, accolades, and activity.

As you gather content to include in your EPK, don't skimp on quality. Poor images will only downgrade the impact of your beautiful press kit. Also, note that because your EPK will likely include many high-resolution images, your end result will be a large PDF file. If it's more than 10MB, don't send as an attachment. Instead, use a file transfer service like WeTransfer and share as a downloadable link.

For example EPK's, visit: www.TenTopTensBook.com/references

Your materials should always be as current as possible. Make it a practice to review your resumé, demo, and EPK on a monthly or bi-monthly basis. And always update your online casting profiles immediately after booking a job, starting a new class or adding an exciting new skill.

4

Top 10
Audition Prep Tips

> "
>
> You're not going
> there to get a job.
> You're going there
> to present what
> you do.

BRYAN CRANSTON

Preparing for an audition involves more than just learning your sides. There are several additional actions you can take to increase your chances of booking the room and booking the job!

1

Take Audition Technique Classes

Hopefully, when you're ready to put yourself out there in the industry, you've taken a range of classes and done your homework to hone your craft. The most immersive acting classes and schools focus on scene study, character breakdown, improv, script analysis, and memorization tools: all the components needed to take on a variety of complex and juicy roles and deliver an amazing performance.

But first, you must book the role, which means winning over the casting director, producers and directors in the audition room.

I've encountered many outstanding actors who simply could not convert an audition into a booking. If your auditions aren't making the strongest impression possible, you won't book the roles you want. Even more damaging, a casting director may not want to bring you in for another audition.

I cannot recommend highly enough the value of taking an Audition Technique class. This is where you'll learn how to make a positive, lasting impression with skills such as how to enter the room and introduce yourself, understanding your best angles, and how to work with the camera and your eye-line. In addition, you'll learn techniques for cold reading, what to do if you mess up in the middle of a scene, staying relaxed in front of a group of strangers, and other essential auditioning fundamentals. These skills will not only improve your chances of a booking but will make you more confident and comfortable in the audition room… often half the battle.

2

Know Who You Are as an Actor

Understanding your type – or as I like to call it, your "Actor Identity" – is one of the most important concepts for any actor to understand about themselves. A strong actor is well trained, having been through extensive schooling to perfect their acting skills. Most likely you've stretched your acting muscles by performing a wide variety of roles – drama and comedy, bad guy to nice guy, sexy girl and unassuming girl next door… rough, light, dry, broad, and everywhere in between. This practice of taking on a range of characters and working through them produces a wonderful actor. However, when trying to make a name for yourself in the industry, focusing on your identity as an actor – your niche – is extremely important.

One of my favorite quotes is "Focus Produces Velocity." When you can concisely understand your category and the range of roles that will most likely get you noticed, you can focus on marketing yourself that way. The "I can play anything" mentality tends to confuse casting directors. Conversely, submitting and pushing for roles that are in a tighter range will give casting a better understanding of where you will fit within their projects.

You may think this approach is limiting but consider actors who've started out in a particular genre and, as they gained notoriety and proved themselves time and again, were then able to broaden into other roles.

One of my favorite examples of this is Jim Carrey. Being cast in the sketch comedy series In Living Color put him on the map by utilizing his incredible physical comedy skills. His success in that show then earned him leading roles in films like Ace Ventura: Pet Detective, Dumb & Dumber, and The Cable Guy. He became a star, and when you're a star you can more easily begin to branch out into other genres and character types because of your notoriety, and the ability to be more selective about the projects you choose. Jim Carrey has since gone on to star in dramatic films such as Eternal Sunshine of the Spotless Mind, The Truman Show and Man on the Moon, to name a few.

There's another way I like to think of it. We've all heard the phrase "jack of all trades, master of none." Your goal should be to become the master of your niche. By understanding your Actor Identity, you can concentrate on the best of who you are as an actor, thus accelerating your career.

Do Your Research

Before every audition, it's essential you research everything you can about the project you're auditioning for. There's so much information at your fingertips online or that your agent/manager can provide, there's no excuse for being uninformed.

◊ If your audition is for a TV show, try to find out who the director is and what other shows s/he has directed. Do they have a consistent style?

◊ Have you seen the show before? If not, go online and watch clips or episodes to understand the tone and style.

◊ Who's opposite in your scenes? If you know the character and who's playing it, you can make stronger, more appropriate choices for the scene.

◊ If auditioning for a comedy, is it single or multi-cam? (More on this in the next section.)

◊ Who are you reading for? Will the producers or director be in the room, or just the casting director?

◊ Is there a script available? If so, READ IT.

When you're more informed you'll feel much more confident about the choices you make and the audition you deliver.

Understand Single-Cam vs. Multi-Cam

In the television comedy world, most shows are either Single Camera (one camera shooting one scene at a time) or Multi-Camera (multiple cameras shooting the same scene from different angles). The direction and style of shows can be drastically different based on these camera set-ups. It's really important to understand which type you're auditioning for because this will affect your choices and delivery.

Single camera shows (Modern Family, New Girl, The Office) tend to feel more realistic and the jokes don't follow the "set-up, punch-line" format. They don't have a laugh track and aren't filmed in front of a live studio audience.

Multi-camera shows (How I Met Your Mother, Big Bang Theory, Friends) are a more traditional sitcom format with a laugh track or audience and tend to follow the "set-up, punch-line" format. It's important for you to understand how to time the jokes, wait for the audience laughter, and feel the rhythm of the dialogue to bring a great performance to a multi-cam show. I highly recommend taking a multi-cam acting class.

5

Have a Great Acting Coach on Standby

I cannot stress enough the importance and benefit of coaching, especially for the big juicy roles every actor wants to book. Every audition is an opportunity to create a new relationship, make a lasting impression, and ideally book a job. Sharing your best performance should be your ultimate goal, so why wouldn't you do all you can to knock it out of the park? Even the most talented and elite actors will prepare for an audition with a coach.

This is not the time to let your ego take control. The attitude that you don't "need" coaching will only sabotage your growth as an actor. You'll never know how much better you could have been had you gone that extra mile.

Ask your agent, manager, and peers for coach recommendations. Most acting teachers offer coaching services as well. Have a few options in case your go-to person isn't available.

Avoid Over Preparing

Getting an audition is exciting. Reading through your sides for the first time is like feeling a new character unfold inside you. It's tempting to spend all your free time getting in touch with the role, who the character is, their back story, memorizing lines, breaking down the scene, playing with beats and timing, and rehearsing, rehearsing, rehearsing. While I encourage every actor to give plenty of time to memorization, preparation and coaching, I think it is equally as important to know when to stop.

There is a point where you can over-rehearse the scene and get so committed to your choices that any change or adjustment can completely throw you off your game. It's much more important to feel comfortable and confident. Don't let the material become so cemented in your head that you can't take a redirect... or worse, cause you to freeze-up when there's a last-minute change in the dialogue. Put your attention on understanding the essence of the character and you'll be a flexible actor in the room.

The Great Equalizer: The Waiting Room

There will be a day when you find yourself in the audition waiting room with other actors you recognize from TV and movies, actors with much bigger resumes than you. You may naturally feel star-struck and intimidated. Or, you might find everyone looks similar to you. Even more confounding, you're the only one of your type. These are all external distractions that can get you worked up and affect your confidence. It's important to remember that you are there because you were chosen to audition for the part, just like the others. Auditions are an equalizer: every actor, no matter how famous, has to prove they're the right actor for the role.

8

Give Your Gift

"The purpose of life is to discover your gift. The meaning of life is to give your gift away." — David Viscott

You are an actor and actors thrive on performing for others. It's your gift to the world. As you prepare for your audition, believe that your choices and performance are your gift and through your preparation, you are wrapping this beautiful gift in the most special paper and gorgeous ribbon you can find. Bring this gift to the audition and hand it over freely, without any expectation of something in return. What you will receive, may surprise you.

9

Don't Seem Desperate

Auditions are precious and for actors, early in their career, they can be few and far between. While you may put a lot of weight on that one audition because of the great opportunity it represents, be careful not to have a life or death attitude about it. No matter how badly you want it, or how badly you need the money, desperation in the audition room is palpable. Casting directors can feel it from the moment you walk in– it changes the energy and the dynamic between you and them. And most importantly, it effects your performance. You'll be so focused on giving them what you think they want that you'll be unable to give an authentic performance with choices that are uniquely yours. Letting go of whatever the audition outcome might be will help you relax, feel more comfortable in the room, and put everyone at ease.

I've had multiple clients tell stories about being at an audition and having it feel "off." In almost every one of these cases, the actor ended up booking the job. Upon reflection, the circumstances that caused them to feel off (whether it be illness, under preparation, etc.) actually caused them to relax and shed desperate energy, unbeknownst to them. The idea is to be aware of when that desperate energy starts to surface and learn to relax and embrace whatever results may come.

Remember, it's not always about booking the role, it's about booking the room. The goal is to create a lasting relationship and leave a strong impression so you are called in by that casting director in the future. Letting go of the frenetic energy that comes from desperation will free you from the pressure you've put on yourself and you'll most definitely deliver a stronger audition.

Don't Obsess About a Role

Sometimes an audition comes along for a totally awesome project and a "put-you-on-the-map" kind of role. It's easy to start obsessing about how your life would change if you book the role: all the attention you might get, the parties you'll be invited to, the talk-shows you could be on, and all the money you could make.

There is danger in this. Not only will you be approaching your audition prep from a place of desperation, but if you don't get the role, the let-down will feel even greater, the feeling of self-defeat even stronger. This can be damaging to your self-confidence.

A pilot test is a perfect example of how this can happen. During the test process, the entire series deal is negotiated before you know if you booked the part. These deals can be for large sums of money, so it's natural to start thinking about your new financially easy life. Even for myself, as an agent, I start dreaming about all the amazing opportunities that may come to my client as a result of booking the pilot.

Letting go of a particular outcome and not attaching yourself emotionally is challenging. It's also a healthy practice for mastering the mental game of your acting career. Instead of obsessing, be passionate about the opportunity. Take satisfaction and energy from that, and then you can't lose.

Plan Your Route

Knowing exactly where your audition is and how long it will take to get there will give you some extra peace of mind so you can focus on the important stuff. This may seem basic and obvious, but I've seen it happen way too often with actors who didn't plan properly and brought a panic energy into the audition because they were rushed and late. In a worst-case scenario, an actor can even miss the opportunity completely by arriving after the audition window has closed. Believe me: it happens. Imagine: all your hard work and you didn't get to share your performance because of poor planning. So:

◊ Map your route online or with an app. Whether you're driving yourself or taking public transportation, don't wait until a couple of hours before your audition to plan your route. Consider the time of day and your method of transportation. L.A. is a big, widespread city and it's entirely possible it could take you an hour or more to get to an audition depending on location, time of day, and traffic. In NYC, subway or bus transfers can add on time. If you're taking a taxi or Uber during rush hour, it may take a long time to find one available and then another long time to get there.

◊ Figure out your parking options. Some casting offices and studio lots will provide parking, but don't assume. For a first call audition, you might be relegated to street parking. Also, not all casting offices will provide parking validation. If your audition information does not come with parking instructions, it's okay to ask.

◊ Keep meter money with you at all times (some meters still only take coins)

Presentation Matters

Of course, you want to make the best impression in the room, so make sure you put thought into your appearance as well.

Avoid wearing any cologne, perfume, scented lotions, or any other strong aromatics. Deodorant good, intense fragrances bad. Someone in the room may have an allergy or sensitivity... or they may just flat out not like the smell of your perfume. You could be wearing the same cologne the casting director's ex-boyfriend wore and they just broke up and she's very emotional and before you know it, you've made her cry before you even did your scene... You get the idea.

Put some thought into your outfit and grooming. Avoid coming into the room looking like you just rolled out of bed (unless the character calls for it). Taking the time to consider your image will tell them you really care about this opportunity.

Avoid jewelry and accessories that make even the smallest amount of noise (dangly earrings, bracelets, big necklaces, certain fabrics). The camera will pick up the sound and it will be distracting on the video.

Make sure your outfit doesn't pull focus from your acting. This is an acting audition, not a modeling go-see. By all means, dress for the character if you choose, but use discretion. If your outfit is overly sexy, distasteful, has graphics that offend, is tight in the wrong places, then they won't notice your acting ability because they're too sidetracked by your wardrobe mishap.

5 Top 10 Business Skills To Apply To Your Career

> ## "
>
> 'May the Force be with you' is charming but it's not important. What's important is that you become the Force – for yourself and perhaps for other people.

HARRISON FORD

I've never been to business school and probably most of you haven't either. And I bet when you decided to pursue a career in acting, you didn't think about business training as part of your required courses. Most artists chose a creative profession to avoid something so left-brained. Well, like it or not, you have chosen to go into business: the "business" of YOU. Implement these simple and pro-active business-minded practices and you will inevitably experience more success and feel more in control of your career.

Keep Track of Your Relationships

A repeated theme in this book is the importance of building your network and relationships. They are key in creating opportunities for yourself. You must nurture those relationships respectfully and selflessly. Keeping track of when and where you met someone, what you discussed, their contact info, and having a follow-up plan are essential for growing your business. I recommend using a spreadsheet that you maintain and utilize regularly. And, to make it easier, I have created one for you!

Template 1 - Relationship Tracker
bit.ly/relationship-tracker

Download the Google Sheets Relationship Tracker at the link above. Click on File, then "Download".

The most important rule in following up with and nurturing relationships is to keep them genuine and generous. Approach people with gratitude and offer them something instead of always asking for something. Imagine having a friend who always wants something from you. It's a one-sided relationship which likely won't last and doesn't feel very good. Find a common connection and have the mindset of "What can I do for you?" instead of "What can you do for me?"

Maintain a Positive Reputation

For any business, a company's reputation can make or break them. It's the cornerstone of success and can outlast any financial fluctuations, successes, or failures. Reputation also influences the type of employees and customers a business attracts. All this seems fairly obvious from a consumer perspective: we buy from companies whose products we like and whose reputations we see as positive.

As the CEO of your "acting business," it's crucial to be aware of your own reputation. Here are a few simple ways to ensure you are maintaining a positive one:

◊ Be nice to everyone on set, from the director to the PA making coffee runs (especially that gal/guy). One negative incident when you weren't kind or respectful to a member of the crew or cast can rapidly spread and characterize you as being difficult, bitchy, hard to work with or any number of unfavorable labels.

◊ Be respectful to other actors in the casting lobby. Being with other actors competing for the same role can create for an emotionally charged environment. It won't help you to show disrespect to your peers. It's unprofessional and a casting assistant will likely overhear and take note. Any negative behavior can affect whether casting considers you as a choice for the job.

◊ Be conscious of your public voice. Social media platforms have provided us all with a new kind of stage where our voices carry further than ever before. Thus, when you pronounce your opinions and beliefs on social media, it's important to think about how they'll affect your reputation. You may end up discouraging people from wanting to hire you if your self-expression offends or insults.

Make Business Cards

Having a business card is a no-brainer for most companies and businesses, but actors rarely consider them a necessity. It's not practical to keep a headshot and resume in your purse or wallet, yet you never know when you might meet someone who wants to stay in contact with you and see your body of work. A business card is the answer!

These days, business cards are very inexpensive to print, and there are plenty of online resources to design your own. Your card should include a headshot photo, name, website, social media, email, phone number, and your agent and/or manager's contact info. DO NOT INCLUDE YOUR PERSONAL ADDRESS.

I've seen some very fun and creative actor business cards. You can go to: Google "actor business card images" for inspiration. Here are a few online resources for designing your own:

◊ Moo.com

◊ VistaPrint.com

◊ JukeBoxPrint.com

◊ Zazzle.com

Keep an Audition Log

Every audition, whether you book the job or not, is an opportunity to learn and grow from your experience. Keeping track of all your auditions, workshops, who you read for, what you wore, the choices you made in the scene, what felt good, what felt not so good, casting director feedback*, whether you got a callback, where to park and if you were on time or not… are all excellent pieces of data for future reference. The next time you go in for the same casting director you'll be a step ahead and may improve your chances of booking by reflecting on what went well before or what not to repeat. It's time for another spreadsheet!

    Template 2 - Audition Log
bit.ly/audition-log

Download the Google Sheets Audition Log at the link above. Click on File, then "Download".

A note about feedback. It can be very difficult to get constructive and detailed feedback about your audition. Casting directors seldom give you much in the room. They are understandably busy and simply don't have time to provide thorough notes about every actor's audition. When they do, you might hear: "They did a great job but we just went another direction"; "Liked her, but not right for this role"; "Did okay, but came off as green"; "Good job, we sent her tape to producers." Often, even your agent or manager won't get the helpful feedback you're craving.

Not knowing how you did in an audition can be frustrating. Everyone wants validation, if only to know whether you're on the right track. My best advice is to validate yourself. You cannot control the opinions of others so don't let them have that power over you. Be realistic, trust your instincts and be honest with yourself about your performance. You have to learn to give yourself constructive feedback.

5

Read the Trades

Almost every industry has their own trade publications. Would you believe there's an "Elevator World," "Onion World," "Parking Today," and "International Sandwich & Snack News?" The entertainment industry has quite a few and you should read them regularly. You'll gain a broader perspective of your industry: the latest projects in development, casting news, staffing changes, pilot pick-ups, series cancellations and everything in-between. Knowing the current trends and direction of your industry can inform the decisions you make about your business and career. Here are some of the essential trade publications to keep bookmarked in your browser:

◊ Deadline Hollywood - deadline.com

◊ Hollywood Reporter - hollywoodreporter.com

◊ Variety - variety.com

◊ IMDB - imdb.com or imdbpro.com

◊ Backstage - backstage.com

◊ The Futon Critic - thefutoncritic.com

◊ Filmmaker Magazine - filmmakermagazine.com

◊ Screen Daily - screendaily.com

◊ TV Week - tvweek.com

◊ American Theatre - americantheatre.org

◊ Broadway - broadway.com and broadway.org

◊ Playbill - playbill.com

◊ Broadway World - broadwayworld.com

Stay Involved in the Unions

SAG-AFTRA (Film/TV/Commercials) and Actor's Equity/AEA (Theater) are the two primary unions for actors. Whether you're a member or not, stay engaged and involved in what's happening at the union level. The unions are there to help regulate and protect your rates and working conditions. They bargain on behalf of you with producers, studios, ad agencies and theater owners. It's important for actors to stay proactive, expressing the needs and desires of the acting community so the unions can support your position and fight for the issues affecting members (or soon-to-be members) like you.

Read their newsletters, visit their websites frequently and vote in leadership elections and ratification of new contracts.

◊ sagaftra.org

7

Never Sign a Contract Without Reviewing

Several years ago, one of my clients was on set shooting a music video. The turnaround time from booking to shoot was less than 12 hours so I did not have time to review the contract prior to my client being on set. This is common with short notice, so I told the producers I would allow the client to report to set and would review the contract in good faith the same day so the production would not be stalled. The client agreed as well. However, upon arrival, the client was approached with a contract and persuaded by the producers to sign as though it had already been approved. This took away all my leverage to negotiate better terms or make my client aware of any rights he was signing away. In this particular case, I would have negotiated a buyout fee, making my client more money for the job.

Without an agent, manager, or attorney's proper review of your contract, you cannot be certain the terms are consistent with what was negotiated or that there aren't new terms and conditions being introduced. You want to make sure you fully understand what you're signing.

Not every producer will provide a contract to the agent ahead of time, especially for standard day-player bookings. There is a certain level of trust between agent and producer that a proper contract will be provided to the client on set. Nonetheless, it's best to always email your agent or manager a picture of the contract to insure it's the correct document. While most of the time the contract is accurate, I've had several incidents where corrections were required.

It can be intimidating if someone from production is pressuring you to sign a contract but remember that you have a legal right to properly review and understand what you're signing. The best way to handle this scenario is to simply ask them to send it to your agent for review. If they won't, then request time to read the contract (no one can expect you to sign anything you haven't read) and call your agent.

Continuing Education – ABL

Always Be Learning!

For a business to maintain its success and grow it must stay relevant and competitive. Staying relevant means educating yourself on how your industry is changing and evolving: What new technologies are changing or disrupting the industry? What new skills are required to stay competitive? How can you grow your brand to stand out among the rest? For an actor, your continued education can take many forms:

◊ Acting classes

◊ Private coaching

◊ Improv and/or comedy classes

◊ Voice lessons

◊ Dance classes

◊ Learn a new language

◊ Dialect training

◊ Stunt training

◊ Production skills (work on "the other side" of the camera)

◊ Watch classic movies & TV

◊ Read/go to plays

◊ Psychology course

◊ Creative Writing course

◊ Social Media course

◊ Casting Office internship

◊ Shadow a director

◊ Money management

◊ Business classes

◊ Marketing

◊ NLP classes

◊ Directing classes

I once interviewed a young actor who told me he'd done all the classes he ever needed. It was as if there was a finite amount of training to do and, since he'd completed a series of courses, there was no need to keep learning. Clearly he did not understand his capacity for growth. Needless to say, I didn't sign him and I certainly haven't seen him on TV or in movies.

9

Create Your Own Pitch

Any good salesman has a well thought out, intriguing, to-the-point sales pitch to entice people to buy their product. It's an essential sales tool. Agents and managers spend most of their workdays crafting pitches to a casting director or producer they want their client to meet. But if there's one person who should know how to pitch you the best, it's YOU! This is also often the hardest thing for many actors to do. To learn how to create your own pitch, read Chapter 7: "Top 10 Strategies for Getting an Agent."

As you create your pitch, ask yourself: "Is this pitch unique to me? Am I being descriptive enough to set myself apart from others?" Every business owner needs to know how to sell their product, so focus on the best way to sell yourself. Share it with your reps so they can more effectively market you.

This is also a great opportunity to analyze whether you are living up to your pitch. Is how you describe your "product" actually what you are "manufacturing?" You may need to adjust your pitch or adjust your image and actor identity if it doesn't match the truth in your pitch.

The "Actor's Car Kit"

In a traditional business, meetings are scheduled with enough time in advance to prepare. In your business, you never know when a last minute, same-day audition might pop up. What if you don't have time to go home to prepare? Keeping a kit in your car stocked with everything you need to feel prepared will ensure you don't sweat when the pressure is on or miss out on an opportunity altogether. Here's a recommended list of essentials to complete your kit:

◊ Headshots/Resumes

◊ Business cards

◊ Make-up basics

◊ Facial wipes

◊ Hairbrush

◊ Hairspray

◊ Hair rubber bands

◊ High heels

◊ Suit jacket (super handy for any roles from upscale to business, to doctor or professional)

◊ Highlighter for sides

◊ Deodorant

◊ Mints

◊ Bottled Water

◊ Quarters (for meters that don't take credit cards)

◊ Black tank top (great for any audition needing to see your physique and for ladies it doubles if you need to look on the sexier side.

6

Top 10
Tech Tools & Tips

"

Tweeting is
like sending
out cool
telegrams to
your friends
once a week.

TOM HANKS

I understand there are some of you who may want to skip this chapter. Embracing technology is not easy for everyone. But I assure you, the tools in this section do not require a degree from MIT to figure out and can be crucial in building your career and brand as an actor. REMEMBER, you are a BUSINESS and anyone owning a business, wouldn't dream of excluding these tools and practices in a plan for growth.

Online Subscriptions & Trades

News Sites - There are several trade websites that are essential for keeping up with the latest entertainment news. Staying informed is necessary if you want to be a savvy and business-minded actor. It's that old cliché that knowledge is power. If the site allows you to subscribe, sign up! Most are free, as are the corresponding smart phone apps, so there's no excuse for not keeping up with breaking news. Here are some of the top entertainment news sites:

◊ DeadlineHollywood.com

◊ HollywoodReporter.com

◊ Variety.com

◊ Playbill.com

◊ Broadway.com

◊ Theatermania.com

IMDBPro - In addition to news sites, you'll want to have an IMDBPro. com account. This Internet Movie Database has become the largest encyclopedia for all things showbiz. Want to see who directed a particular film? See the full cast of a show? Explore a talent agency's roster? It's all here. There's a lot of information available on the public version of the site, but as a professional actor, you will absolutely want to spend the extra money to register for an IMDBPro account. You'll be able to update your own profile, as well as see information not available to the public —contact information for production companies, representatives, publicists, attorneys, casting directors, and more.

Backstage.com – Originally a printed periodical, Backstage's online magazine is a great resource. You'll find helpful advice articles on topics like Auditioning Technique, Headshot Tips, Casting Director Pet Peeves, etc. Additionally, you can sign up for an annual membership and get premium benefits like creating your own profile and browsing their job and audition boards.

Social Media

There's been a lot of emphasis put on the importance of having a large social media following as an actor. Without a doubt, we are living in a time where your voice can be heard by thousands through one simple post. Agencies and firms have launched divisions whose sole purpose is to capitalize on and create empires out of social media entrepreneurs and performers (I've done several deals where the size of an actor's following has become leverage in the negotiation). If you have the capability to reach a large audience, then you become a marketing asset for whatever production has hired you. Because your audience is unique to you, it's more personal and authentic and, thus, your message has a greater impact.

It's important to be responsible about what your audience sees and reads about you and your brand. Build your online reputation through your behavior. Decide if you're willing to commit to growing your audience, or if you just want to participate casually on various social media platforms. Both require you to be thoughtful about what you put out there. If your goal is to grow your audience then you'll want to educate yourself further on the best strategies for growth. If you're not about the numbers, you still need to be well versed in social media etiquette.

Internet & Social Media Do's

MINI TOP 10

1. DO share your opinion thoughtfully and respectfully. If you don't have anything nice to say, don't say it.

2. DO engage and interact with your followers in a positive way. Commenting and posting questions will keep your community loyal and you'll increase your followers through engagement.

3. DO follow others. You've got to give to get.

4. DO share your accomplishments, humbly. Have a great review? Working with an A-lister? Receive a nomination or award? All great things to promote, just do so in an unpretentious way.

5. DO be mindful of proper spelling and grammar. It's simply more professional and gives you more credibility.

6. DO post photos, wisely. Visuals win the day on social media platforms. There's a reason Instagram has more than double the number of users than Twitter.

7. DO use hashtags & tag people, smartly. They should always be relevant to your post.

8. DO give props. Acknowledging and tagging others on social media for something inspiring they did or said shows you are socially aware, promotes positivity, illustrates it's not always about you, and supports the originator.

9. DO vet your friend requests... as much as you can. Even a glimpse at a Facebook page can provide a lot of info about a person. Check if you have mutual friends.

10. DO pay attention to trending hashtags and post something related, but only if it feels genuine and authentic.

Internet and Social Media Dont's

MINI TOP 10

1. DON'T share pictures, call sheets, character details, storylines, or any info related to a project you booked without approval. This is a very serious issue and may result in a lawsuit. No post is worth that.

2. DON'T share the year of your birthday on social media or

public websites. In your business, you don't have an age, you have an age range.

3. DON'T share news stories and links that might offend or ostracize you from people wanting to work with you.

4. DON'T overdo it. Posting and re-tweeting too often has been shown to lead to loss of followers. Quality over quantity.

5. DON'T only promote and market your actor self and acting work. Followers tend to want to know the real person behind the actor. Authenticity is key. Posting about real life keeps you relatable and your followers feeling more connected.

6. DON'T WRITE IN ALL CAPS. As a general rule, you'll be thought of as a screamer. CAPS should be used sparingly and only for specific EMPHASIS.

7. DON'T solicit casting directors or agents on social media. Friend them, engage with them, but don't submit or ask for work.

8. DON'T drink and post. Just like a drunk text, you'll probably write something you regret. Nothing is so important you can't wait until you're sober.

9. DON'T post photos you don't want to live on the internet FOREVER... ANYWHERE. A simple copy and paste means your photos can be used by anyone. Be smart about posting compromising and promiscuous pictures. It can make or break your career.

10. DON'T be overly specific about your location. Paparazzi and stalker alert: It's always safest to simply say you are in Hawaii, rather than the exact resort you are staying at. Another great practice for when you are a superstar!

5

Facebook Fan Page

Consider separating your personal Facebook page from your professional one by creating a Fan Page dedicated to all things related to your career. I talk a fair amount in this book about treating your career like a business. As your star rises, the desire to separate your private life from your public life will grow stronger. Drawing those lines early on is important. Having a fan page creates a perception that your career is at a higher level and serves as a promotional platform for all your acting news and events.

Website & Domain Name

A website is an essential marketing tool. If you owned any other business, you wouldn't think twice about creating a website. Your profession is no different. A website is the best place to share news, photos, demo reels, your resumé and any other audio/visuals. You control the look and feel so your site reflects your personality and your brand. And, the best part is that you can build a site relatively inexpensively. It no longer takes a professional web designer to create one for you. There are several template-based, website building tools online these days which make it fun and easy for you. The top three DIY website builders are:

◊ www.wix.com

◊ www.squarespace.com

◊ www.editorx.com

Even if you aren't building a website right now, start the process by purchasing your domain name. Having your own official website is a great idea whether you're famous or not... but it will be very important the more well-known you become. I'm sure you've heard stories about celebrity websites that seem authentic when, in actuality, it's some crazy fan imposter posting unauthorized, unauthenticated, or unflattering content. Don't let that happen to you. Domain names are relatively cheap ($10-20/year). You can inexpensively purchase several versions of your name and several domain extensions (.com, .net, .org, .biz, etc) from sites like GoDaddy, HostGator, BlueHost, etc. This will ensure no one else can own your name, create a fake website, or charge you an outrageous price to buy back your named domain.

Google Yourself Regularly

When any of us are in the market to buy a new product, what do we often do? An internet search for reviews on said product. If we see enough bad reviews, we're probably not going to buy the product. As an actor, the same rings true for you. Google yourself and see what comes up.

Disney is a perfect example of a company concerned with hiring talent who align with their brand. Their audience is made up of children, teens and families and they take care not to hire talent who may be perceived to have unsavory values or engage in questionable behavior which might deter their target audience. Try Googling not only your "FULL NAME", but also "Photos of FULL NAME", "actor FULL NAME", "LEGAL NAME," etc. Do the same in other search engines like Bing and Yahoo. They may yield different results. Having control of your online presence is essential for your business and your brand. If you are on websites that are unfavorable, look into how you can remove yourself or disassociate yourself. Don't give anyone a reason not to "buy" you!

8

Consider Starting a YouTube Channel

Consider Starting a YouTube Channel I'm not suggesting you turn yourself into a "YouTuber," unless that's your dream. However, there are some benefits for having a YouTube (YT) presence.

It's a smart place to host your demo reel and show "permissible" scenes and footage of your work. YT videos perform better in Google searches. This is because Google owns YT, thus they have better SEO (search engine optimization). This means that if your demo reel is hosted on YT it will rank higher than if it's hosted on your own website or another site (nine times out of ten, YT videos will rank higher than Vimeo videos and blogs). Nonetheless, I still recommend Vimeo as the go-to home for all your videos and self-tapes because of the ease of downloading. By hosting your reel on your YT channel and Vimeo, you'll be able to maximize exposure.

With a YouTube channel, you can also start to gain subscribers and build your fan base. There may be fans who are more active on YouTube than on Instagram, Facebook, or Twitter, so adding another way for your fans to interact with you and follow you will enhance your overall social media footprint.

When creating your YouTube channel be sure to customize it with images and page art that reflect who you are as an artist. Include links to your other social media channels and your website. And don't forget about an enticing "About" section that shares with your followers a little piece of who you are.

There's so much more to optimizing your YouTube channel, but starting with something basic will ensure you're casting a wide net to reach all corners of the web.

Self-Tape Set-Up

Within the last 5 years, I think it's safe to say that the requests for self-tape auditions has grown exponentially. I think there are three significant reasons for this phenomenon.

1. Runaway production. From Vancouver to Toronto, Portland to Atlanta, Detroit to New Orleans, and everywhere in between, including overseas, the number of TV and Film productions shooting outside of Los Angeles and NY has been on the rise. For example, in 2013, Louisiana was the shoot location for more Top 25 movies than any other location, beating out Los Angeles and Canada.* (*FilmLA, Inc., 2013 Feature Film Production Report, FilmLA Research, Los Angeles; 2014) This has led to a growth in regional actor pools and a decrease of producers located in the major casting hubs of Los Angeles and New York. Consequently, for shows and movies shooting on location, the producers are rarely in the room with actors for auditions or callbacks. Self-taping has become the equivalent of going into a casting office and being put on tape for the producers.

2. Technology. The fact that high quality movies can now be shot on a smart phone means it's easier and cheaper than

ever to produce a self-tape audition. Additionally, file transfer sites have taken the pain and frustration out of sending large video files.

3. Budget. Tightening of budgets and an increase in the amount of content means there may not always be a budget for a casting studio for in-room auditions. Often the pressure to cast a project quickly means fewer casting sessions, so the solution to seeing more actors for any given role is to request self-tapes.

As an agent, the now widespread acceptance of self-tapes has provided us with an additional tool to help sell our clients. If casting is not sold on scheduling an appointment, we can often persuade them to see an actor on tape.

Conclusion: Self-tapes have now been so integrated into the casting process that it's a new norm. Amidst the global COVID-19 pandemic, it has been the only safe way to audition actors. While we will get back to in-room auditions, we will never return to the days before the self-tape option.

What does all this mean for you as an actor? You MUST take steps to create a great self-tape "studio" of your own or have on hand a list of companies who provide self-tape services. Don't let a poor self-tape be the reason they chose the other actor!

Here's my go-to checklist for Creating a High Quality Self-Tape Audition:

EQUIPMENT/TECHNICAL

√ Camera & Tripod

A high quality smart phone camera or camcorder. Invest in

a tripod - this will save you from having to find the right surface to prop up your phone or use a stack of books, dresser, coatrack, or the unsteady hands of your roommate or partner. And ALWAYS record in landscape (horizontal) mode unless instructed otherwise.

√ Sound

Make sure the sound quality is excellent. You may have to move closer or reduce background noise (birds chirping outside an open window, wind blowing, a TV on in another room, or even an article of clothing that creates too much noise when you move). Test your voice and your reader's voice before you record your audition. Nothing ruins your hard work more than poor sound quality, so ensuring you can be heard clearly is critical. You might even invest in an external microphone or lavalier mic which clips on your clothes.

√ Environment/Lighting

A suitable environment, preferably indoors, against a plain wall, somewhere neutral where you are well lit, without background noise or echoing. Unless you're creating a specific environment for the take, make sure you are centered, lit from behind the camera (not from behind you, or from the side), and completely in the frame. Typical framing is from your middle, upper arm to a couple inches above your head.

FILMING

√ Read with a Partner

Your partner should be familiar with the material and know how to deliver their lines correctly so the conversation feels authentic. Weak partners can really bring the scene down and detract from your own performance, so your partner should be competent and comfortable.

√ Slate

Make sure you slate at the beginning or end of your audition. Say your name, agency, height if relevant to the role, turn left and right to give both profiles, pan or zoom for a full body shot, and don't be afraid to smile! Slating is a brief way to introduce yourself and shows a flash of personality to fit the moment. Emphasis on brief.

√ Performance

It's perfectly fine to move around and use body language during a take if the scene and the role call for it. Just make sure you stay in frame and keep the attention on your performance. You should be off book for self-tape auditions unless you've had a very quick turnaround.

√ Props

Props can add a layer of realism to a character or scene, especially if the sides refer to specifics. However, be careful about overdoing it. You may choose to do takes with and without, just in case. Avoid any props that distract from your performance, make too much noise, could malfunction, etc. Remember, this is about you, and not what your prop is doing, so when in doubt, go without... or at least do a take without the prop as well. Avoid eating food during your scene, unless essential to the scene.

√ Multiple Takes

Since you aren't in the casting office to get a redirect of your scene, it's often a good idea to do several takes making different choices for your scene.

SENDING

√ Size

As a general rule, aim to make your file no larger than 100MB. Resize the file before sending if needed. This will ensure an easier delivery and viewing process.

√ Format

.MP4, .MOV, .WMV are the best formats.

√ Delivery

Sending video files as attachments should be avoided. It can take forever and some email service providers have a maximum size limit for attachments. Instead, send it by a link or file transfer website such as Hightail, Vimeo, DropBox, and Wetransfer.

Password protect if you are using Vimeo or a similar service. And be sure your video is set to "downloadable". Youtube is not recommended, as they do not have an easy download option.

10

Performer Track

Performer Track is an extremely thorough online software application designed for actors to track all aspects of their career. I have a whole section in this book about applying business strategies to your career, and Performer Track is a tool that can assist with several of these areas. Through the application, you'll be able to track all the details of your auditions, booked jobs, classes, workshops, related expenses, income, contacts, and feedback, while always having access to statistical reports.

It's not free, but in my opinion it's a worthwhile and valuable investment in your career. If you are not an organized person by nature, this will be a lifesaver. www.performertrack.com

7 Top 10 Tips For Getting An Agent

> **"**
>
> Like any other actor, my agent called me with an opportunity. It just so happens that the opportunity was the lead in 'Star Wars.'

JOHN BOYEGA

Signing with an agent is a hugely significant step in any actor's career. It signals that you are a professional and opens the door to so many opportunities. It's no wonder that the single most common question I get asked by unrepresented actors is "How do I get an agent?" While timing and relationships are huge factors, there are also several proactive things you can do to improve your chances of attracting an agent and persuading them to work with you.

1

Find Opportunities To Showcase Your Talent

Seeing is believing. Acting is a visual and experiential art form – no news there. The only way to know if you're any good is to see you in action. If you don't have a demo reel that shows off your work, then you'll need to look for other opportunities to showcase your talent.

Class Showcases - many acting programs culminate in a performance for industry professionals, including agents, managers, and casting directors. When vetting an acting school, consider one that produces such an event.

One-Time Workshops - There has been much controversy over the ethics of fee-based Actor Workshops designed to provide an outlet for actors to perform in front of agents, managers and casting directors ("Observers"). When the popularity of these types of workshops increased, so did the number of businesses wanting to get in on the action. Unfortunately, many of them were formed solely to capitalize on and take advantage of desperate actors. A workshop should never be a "pay to audition" opportunity and should always include some form of interaction with and education from the Observers. Luckily, as a result of California state legal action in 2016 & 2017, there has been a crackdown on businesses operating in violation of the Krekorian Talent Scam Prevention Act. As a result, all workshops must now comply to create a more positive experience for the actors.

When vetting a workshop, my advice is to confirm the following:

◊ The workshop includes an educational component, the opportunity to ask questions and/or actually converse with the Observers.

◊ You will receive feedback from the Observers in some form, whether written or verbal.

◊ You have the option of providing your own material & reader, so you can really shine.

◊ They provide a way to follow up with the Observers.

◊ Workshops in California are bonded* by the State Labor Commission.

If you enjoy reading state bills and laws, and want to learn more about the Krekorian Act, here's a link to the bill: www.bit.ly/Krekorian-Act

Free Shows - Everyone loves free stuff. If you're in a play or show that you are particularly proud of that showcases your talents, consider providing comp tickets to reps. Do an email or postcard campaign promoting the show, along with an invitation to come and see you in it, your treat. Remember to personalize the invitation!

Top 10 Pro Tip: Provide 2 tickets instead of one. So many times I've receive an invitation to see someone in a show but they provide only one ticket. While I've certainly attended many shows solo, you are much more likely to get someone to attend if they can bring a date/friend along.

Network Showcases - Every year, the major television networks (CBS, NBC, ABC) produce showcases. They invest time and money into grooming a select group of actors to present to their network executive, producers and casting teams. But other industry professionals are also invited to attend so the audience is chock full of people who might have influence over your career, including agents.

The casting process for these showcases is lengthy and they look at actors at every level of their career, from all over the country, and from an array of diverse backgrounds. Hundreds, if not thousands, of actors apply to be chosen as part of the cast. Being selected is a major feather in your cap and the exposure can be priceless. If you are currently represented, your agent or manager will know how to submit you. If not, the showcases always release their breakdown on Actors Access so you can submit yourself.

2

Target Specific Agencies

At least once a week I get an email from someone asking me for literary representation or I get sent a script for shopping around. The only problem is that I'm not a literary agent. A little bit of Googling would have saved them the trouble.

It's important to do your research and target specific agents and agencies you think would be a good fit. I know many of you are itching to sign with ANY agency, but I still urge you to do the proper research and target agencies based on your individual career needs. Ending up at an agency that is not a good fit doesn't benefit you in the long run and could actually cost you time and money. Indicating to a prospective agent that you've done your research and feel like their agency is a good fit also suggests you're a smart, resourceful actor who takes their career seriously.

Consider the following criteria as you compile your target list:

◊ Does the agent/agency represent all ages, specifically your age?

◊ Do they have a specialty? (comedians, personalities, kids, alternative types, diversity, social media influencers, etc.)

◊ What is their roster to rep ratio? Does it look like there are enough agents to handle the size of their client list?

◊ Where are they located? Is the distance you would need to travel for a face to face meeting important to you?

◊ Do they have multiple locations within the U.S? Internationally?

◊ Are you at a place in your career that aligns with the caliber of talent on their existing roster? (You can get lost in a sea of actors if the agents are primarily focused on their heavy hitters.)

◊ Do they have a good reputation?

◊ Do they have a professional image and respectable online presence?

You can find most of these answers on IMDBPro and the web. You can also ask your community of actors, teachers, and coaches for their opinion. Learning from other people's personal experience is invaluable.

3

Research Submission Policies

Now that you have a well-researched target list, it's time to investigate the submission policies of each agency. This is a simple and logical exercise, yet many actors make the mistake of not learning the submission criteria of the agency to which they are applying. Either they'll send a submission for the wrong kind of representation (remember all those literary rep emails I get?), or they send in their materials without regard to the agency's requirements.

If you want your materials to have the best odds at being considered, find out the agency's preferred submission method. Some may prefer emails only and have very specific instructions on what to include. Some may accept hard copy submissions but they may need to be addressed to a particular individual or department. Headshots, demo reels, postage, cover letters all cost money. Armed with this knowledge, you will also lessen the impact on your wallet and reduce the amount of waste (a lot of submissions go right in the trash… harsh truth).

Some agencies may not accept unsolicited submissions. An unsolicited submission means it was not requested or referred by an acceptable source. In these instances, you'll need to find someone connected to the agency who can put in a good word or help get your materials into the hands of the targeted individual. Existing clients, acting teachers, managers, and casting directors are all people who could potentially help. More about that below.

An agency's website may include their submission policy, or you may simply need to call and ask. Take the time to do so. It's worth it!

4

Ask For Referrals

You have your target list of agencies and have investigated their submission policies. So what more can you do to get eyes on your materials?

Relationships are king in this business, as we know. When it comes to piquing the interest of an agent, it's no different. When I get a referral from a casting director, manager, acting coach, director, producer, client, or anyone who's opinion I respect, 100% of the time I will look at the referred actor's materials. A referral tells me that the actor has already impressed one of my colleagues with their work, so I should see what they're all about.

How do you get someone to refer you? First and foremost, you must not be afraid to ask for help. But if you're not comfortable asking a fellow actor to introduce you to their rep, there are other resources. As I mentioned, casting directors, managers, producers, casting coaches, directors, and others in the industry are all potential "angels" to help connect you.

The important thing is to be respectful when you ask. Don't be pushy or overly persistent. When it comes to personal relationships, favors can be sensitive territory, so leave it up to the individual with the connection to decide if they are comfortable making the introduction.

You may need to think outside the box. I once got an actor's materials sent to me from an old boss who became a real estate agent and saw a homebuyer's daughter in a play and agreed to help her by contacting me. You just never know. And you just never know who someone knows. Make it known among your non-industry friends and family that you are looking for an agent because a connection can come from the least obvious place!

5

Create the Perfect Pitch

It's not enough to just send your headshot, resume and demo to your targeted list of agents. You'll need to figure out how to stand out from the crowd. You need to sell yourself! One way to do this is to create an enticing pitch. Throughout this book, I've touched on the importance of understanding who you are as an actor and what you are bringing to the table. Now it's time to put it on paper (er... email). Here are my tips on creating a strong pitch.

√ Personalize it.

Nine times out of 10, if I receive a new talent submission email and it starts out with "Dear Agent" or "Hi!" without my name, it's going to be deleted. I've also been addressed by names other than my own. We understand you probably created a template email to blast out, but it shouldn't feel like a mass email. This is not the time for MailChimp. It's a turn off and says you lack a level of care about the email and haven't done your homework about the agent you're addressing.

√ Tell us why.

Mention briefly why you want to be represented by that particular agency. Again, this says that you've been proactive in your research. It's also another way to make it feel more personal.

√ State your purpose.

While it may seem obvious, let us know what type of representation you are looking for so we know you've landed in the right inbox.

√ Get to the meat.

An agent's eye is going to make a beeline for your credits and achievements, so get to it right away. Your life story and bio might be fascinating, but attach it in a word doc, or provide a website link. If you must, choose just a couple enticing personal facts.

√ List it.

A list format creates for an easier read. It breaks up blocks of text and attracts attention. If I receive an email that looks like a novel, I'm turned off from reading it. But a list, I love! (Can you tell?) Include only the highlights. Your resume is included if we want to see the full breadth of your experience. The pitch should point out your most significant work. The following are some examples of highlights you can grab to make your list pop.

- Drop some names of people you've worked with. This is the time to brag.

  Just shot a Supporting role in the Indie feature, "_____" opposite "_____"

> *Played the Lead in a web pilot, "_____",*
> *directed by Larry David (Seinfeld, Curb Your*
> *Enthusiasm)*

- Include details that provide context and allure about a particular credit. This is especially helpful for projects that are lesser known.

> *Co-Lead in "_____" which just won the*
> *Audience Award at the Tribeca Film Festival.*

> *Booked a Guest Star on "_____" via direct*
> *offer.*

> *Nominated/Won Best Actor for my performance in*
> *"_____" at SXSW.*

- Include significant Training, Graduations, Awards, & Achievements.

> *Graduated Groundlings Level 3*

> *MFA from NYU Tisch*

> *3 years private coaching with Anthony Meindl*

- Prototypes - you should have a good handle on your type and brand by now. Tell us that you understand your niche by including a few character traits and prototypes so we start to create a picture of who you are.

- Noteworthy Skills - what are your major assets when it comes to your skillset? List a few that might entice an agent.

Fluent in 3 languages - English, Spanish, & Arabic
Certified Stunt Performer

Black belt in Karate

Dual citizenship - Canadian with U.S. Green Card
or Visa

- Look beyond the resumé. Think about things you are proud of that may not have a place on your resumé in the form of a credit, skill or training.

    Tested last pilot season for the FOX sitcom,
    " _____ "

    Was personally requested by director _____
    to audition for " _____ "

    LA Times called my performance in " _____ ",
    "bold, daring, and utterly enthralling".

    Recently signed with manager, _____ at
    _____ .

    Worked as an Intern with _____ casting and
    they always call me in for roles I'm right for.

√ Include referrals.

A "normal" job application would always include a few referrals for their prospective employer as a background check. If you have some influential people rooting for you, and if they agree you can include them as a referral, then go for it.

89

This provides additional credibility and shows that others are confident in your work and willing to put their reputation on the line for you.

√ Spell/Grammar check.

Please have someone spell and grammar check. We're not signing you for your English skills, but it sure is nice when the pitch is well written.

√ Include your materials.

Attachments should be limited to 2 MB in my opinion. It's so easy to resize documents and images, and a huge attachment can freeze computers, or never even reach the intended (depending on your email provider).

- Attach a PDF of your resume, and bio if you have one.

- Include 1-2 headshots. It's also great and eye catching to embed a couple photos in the body of the email.

- Audio and Video files Demo should never be attached. Include web links to download or view instead.

√ Lastly, infuse it with your personality.

This is where you can get creative so the letter doesn't feel stale or like a form letter. Giving it your personal touch will start to bring your words and headshots to life. Have fun with it, particularly if you're a comedic actor... make me believer!

The waiting...

By now, you've researched agencies, sought out referrals, written a killer pitch, and shared your materials. What now? Well, hopefully you'll produce a few meetings from all your hard work. However, agents are busy people, so you may need to do some follow ups. I am often asked, "how soon after sending my materials should I reach back out to an agent?" As a good rule of thumb, I recommend waiting a week. This is a reasonable amount of time for an agent to get caught up on emails. And if they're anything like me, they have a meeting once per week to discuss potentials, so giving it a solid week will allow time for scheduled reviews. A very brief, short and sweet follow-up on your original email is all you need. But, be forewarned, you simply may not hear back. It is not a productive use of an agent's time to respond to every actor submission if they are passing on you. Rest assured, if they're interested, you'll hear about it.

You got an interview!

Incorporate these next tips to ensure you are prepared for your meeting and will win them over!

What's Your Momentum?

Agents love to have exciting things to talk about when it comes to their clients. New bookings, awards, press, anything that sets an actor apart. These noteworthy bits help define an actor's momentum, and when you're looking for representation, your momentum is extremely valuable. Consider the recent work you've done, significant feedback, interviews, accolades and be prepared to talk build those into your pitch. This is one of those times when it's a good idea to name drop. If you recently shot a film and had a scene opposite an A-lister, then let's hear about it. If you received an award that a famous actor has received in the past, then point it out. Agents want to know what makes you special because we have to convince casting directors and producers that you are special. Momentum is contagious. If you're driving a fast-moving train, others will naturally want to get on board!

Talk About Your "Why"

"My desire to become an actor really early on was [that] I wanted to communicate something, to reflect something back to the audience. For me, that was what was powerful. I think that's what's more important than being in the center of the stage. To communicate something" - *Matt Dillon*

Why you do something can be the single most significant driver of success. Passion comes from having a strong "why." I discuss this further, along with creating your personal mission statement, in the Staying Grounded chapter of the book. When I sit down with an actor looking for an agent and they can't tell me why they want to be a successful actor, it makes me question whether they will be motivated enough to make it in such a competitive industry. Conversely, if an actor conveys why they love acting, why they want to succeed, what motivates them, it inspires and motivates me to want to come along for the journey. Just saying that you are an actor because you love it so much isn't enough. Dig deeper. Why do you love it so much?

Any employer wants to hear why you are the best person for the job, what drives you and keeps you going day after day, even when the chips are down. Sharing your "why" also provides a personal insight into who you are and what it will be like to work with you. It humanizes the agent/actor (employer/candidate) dynamic and shifts the conversation from superficial and formal, to personal and relaxed. And, you'll become a more memorable prospect.

Attitude Is Everything

We all know the impact a first impression can make. I can tell in the first 5 minutes of talking to an actor whether I'm interested in working with them. It's crucial to be aware of the energy you give off. It can be the difference between getting an agent or not. On several occasions, I have decided not to sign a very talented actor because my gut told me their personality would present a challenge and likely inhibit our amount of success together.

Be humble, yet confident. There's a fine line between confidence and cockiness. The key is to be humble. Agents want to work with actors who have confidence in their abilities, know how to walk into a casting office exuding self-assurance but, at the same time, show no disrespect or entitlement.

I believe the winning combination is a strong belief in yourself, preparation, and resilience.

People want to work with others who have a healthy self-esteem and belief in themselves. It tells us that we can trust in your abilities, because you do.

Proper preparation is like icing on the confidence cake. The more prepared you are for a meeting or audition, the more your confidence grows.

And resilience is knowing that you can always bake another cake because you have all of the ingredients. You are not immune to the downfalls of the industry, you've been humbled by close calls not going your way or streaks of auditions without booking. Yet, you bounce back each time, confident that there's a win on the horizon... not because you are entitled to it, but because you're doing the work and maintaining the right attitude.

No matter how many auditions you've gone to, there's never an excuse to take an attitude of "you owe me this."

No matter how many roles you've booked or how much praise you've received, there's never a good reason to act like you're better than everyone else.

And no matter how much you think you know, there's always room to grow.

Share Your Pro-Activity

Agents realize that you've come to them to help launch your career. Actors need agents for their resources, support, and expertise. We are the primary facilitators of opportunities for our clients. But actors cannot rely on their agent alone to create opportunities. For some, there is an expectation that once you've signed with an agent, you can sit back and wait for the auditions to roll in. On the contrary, complacency won't get you anywhere, and is reflected in all areas of your career. Actors must look at their career just like any other day job and ask: What am I doing on a daily basis towards building success? The best clients are those who pair their pro-activity with that of their agent.

When meeting with a potential agent, be prepared to talk about the things you're doing on your own and the actions you will continue to do once you've signed with them. Tell them about the action items in this book, for example, that you are implementing to help further your career. Create your own daily practice of being proactive and you'll not only help yourself, you'll inspire your agent to want to work harder for you.

Ask Smart Questions

A meeting for representation might seem like the agent holds all the cards. They ask most of the questions, examine the actor's personality, learn about their experience and aspirations, in order to determine if they're sitting across from a moneymaker. However, the agent/actor meeting is not a one-sided interview. It is an opportunity for both parties to learn whether there is mutual interest and chemistry in working together.

If the agent doesn't ask if you have any questions for them, make sure you take that initiative. Below are some smart questions which will impress the agent, show them you care about learning how they operate and that you understand working together is a mutual decision.

◊ "If I have a connection or lead on a particular project, are you interested in hearing about it?"

◊ "What would your strategy be for an actor with my resume?"

◊ "Are you a member of the Association of Talent Agencies (ATA)? Or, SAG-AFTRA franchised?"

◊ "What type of contract do you ask your clients to sign?"

◊ "How do you prefer to communicate with your clients?"

Avoid asking "Do you have anyone like me?" because we won't even know that until we meet you. The fact that you got a meeting means you've already passed the first hurdle based on physical attributes alone. Most agents are not going to agree to meet with or sign an actor who is too much of a conflict with another client.

--

The process of getting an agent is different for everyone. For some, it happens quickly. For others, it can take years. Be persistent. As good things happen in your career, use those moments and try reaching out to agents again. And keep working on your craft. As your work continues to grow, people will take notice.

8 Top 10 Tips For A Strong Agent Relationship

> ## "
> I wish to be cremated. One tenth of my ashes shall be given to my agent, as written in our contract.
>
> GROUCHO MARX

Your relationship with your agent is one of the most important relationships you will have in your career. There are also a lot of misconceptions and misunderstood expectations about an agent's role in an actor's career. Below are some great ways to stay in your agent's favor and have a balanced and mutually beneficial relationship.

1

Trust Your Agent

Start your relationship with your agent from a place of trust. It's their job to hold your hand and help you achieve success but they can't do that without your trust. Every actor whom an agent has ever represented, every negotiation, every victory, every disappointment provides a reference for how they navigate the industry in the best interest of their clients. This collection of experience and knowledge is how an agent provides you with the best advice and decision-making to help you book work. They know the marketplace. They understand the protocol and hierarchies within the industry. They've seen what works and what doesn't work, so trust them. A good agent will always do their best to guide you in a direction they feel will yield the greatest reward.

I've had clients who constantly resisted my advice, or doubted I was working hard, or worse, thought that I didn't believe in them. Whenever I begin to sense this, it's time for a conversation and often results in discontinuing our relationship. If you're having doubts about your agent, talk to them and express your feelings. But also understand you need to have a lot of trust in them for the relationship to be successful.

Realize You Aren't Their Only Client

In a dream world, I think every agent would only have one client on whom they could focus 100% of their energy and efforts. However, from a business standpoint, that's just not realistic. Most agents do not make enough commission off a single client to be able to sustain a business. It's a balancing act for them to have enough clients to be profitable, while not overloading their roster. Having a variety of clients inherently benefits each individual client because the agency becomes a better resource for casting directors, producers and directors.

You also need to maintain a balance with how and when you communicate with your agent, knowing that they have other clients they're servicing just like you. Calling every day to ask what's going on, bombarding their inbox with emails of projects you've heard about, doubting that they're pitching and pushing for you, will only create distance and you may wind up with no agent at all. A better strategy is to ask your agent how often they like to be contacted, what type of project information they like to know about, and the communication style they prefer. You're a team and agreeing on the rules is going to ensure more wins.

Remember That Your Agent Also Has A Life

Every agent knows their workday doesn't end when the offices closes. Their job requires them to be on call 24/7. However, they all have personal lives outside their career – families, hobbies, dinner parties, errands, vacations, etc. When a client doesn't respect that space, it's frustrating and can lead to a problematic relationship. But you do need a way to contact your agent should there be an on-set emergency or time sensitive issue. Ask them for the best way to make contact after hours in those circumstances. But, first, ask yourself if it's something that can wait until the next morning or after the weekend. Giving them space for their personal lives, makes them happier people in their professional lives.

Check Your Voicemail & Email Frequently

Acting is an unpredictable business. Opportunities can arise at any time – whether it's an audition, an avail check, or an offer. It's also a fast-paced business where timing can mean the difference between getting booked or not. It's crucial that you check your voicemail and email frequently.

On several occasions, I've had actors miss out on a booking because they didn't respond quickly enough about their availability and another actor got the job. Or, there may be important information about an audition which would make or break your chances of booking (ie: location change, time/date change, new sides, updated character description). In this day and age, technology allows us to have immediate contact with one another, which also means there aren't many excuses for not being reachable and up to date.

◊ Always make sure voicemail is set up on your phone, and your mailbox is not full.

◊ Program your emails to be delivered to your smart phone. You may not want to be alerted about every email received, so check if your device has a smart alert so you're pinged only when you receive an email from your rep and members of your team.

◊ Respond in a timely manner and acknowledge receipt of the correspondence. Chasing down confirmation is time consuming and not fun for us.

◊ Notify us if you'll be unreachable for a prolonged period of time and if there's a preferred way to contact you.

5

Don't Ask For Audition Time Frames Unless You Absolutely Need To

While this may seem small, it's actually a very big deal for most agents. Regardless of the type of audition, making calls all day long trying to get time frames or dealing with schedule changes is both tedious and time-consuming. We understand you work hard to make your schedule work and we'd like to have you at the audition, but asking about time frames for every audition should not be a general practice. Our time is better spent trying to get you the actual audition. Clients who consistently have scheduling issues reflect a lower level of commitment to their career and can adversely affect how hard an agent works for them. It's common knowledge that auditions pop up with only a day or two's notice... and sometimes, the same day. It's your responsibility, as a professional actor, to anticipate the spontaneity of the business by keeping a flexible schedule.

Share Your Audition Experiences

I wish I could see video for every one of my clients' auditions but sadly that is not the reality. Obviously, agents are not in the audition room and, apart from self-tapes, an agent rarely sees their clients' auditions. So we rely on you to tell us how things went. What was the reaction from the casting director? How long were you in the room? Did they laugh? Did they cry? Did they redirect you? These bits of info give us an insight into what's happening in the room. It's a challenge to get detailed feedback from a casting director, so your impressions are important and will at least allow us to hear your side of the experience.

We can also pick up on patterns. I've had clients who, whenever they said they felt terrible about an audition, actually booked the job. And when they felt they nailed it and were sure of getting a callback, never did. When we can pick up on these patterns, we can work together to troubleshoot why your auditions aren't converting to bookings. Auditioning is a skill in and of itself. The more agents know about what's happening behind those casting room doors, the more we can help you improve that skill.

Make Your Agent Immediately Aware Of Issues On Set

Your agent is your biggest ally and is there to hold your hand when there's business to be done, contracts to review, unfair practices occurring, or any other scenario in which you find yourself in an uncomfortable position or beyond your expertise.

It's totally normal to feel like you don't want to create waves on set, risk your relationship with anyone in production, or be looked at as a troublemaker. Let your agent do the dirty work. An agent can call a producer and get to the bottom of things. In fact, we are the exact person they expect to hear from when such a situation arises. We fight your fight and keep conflict out of your relationships by being the bad guy, if needed.

Here are a few examples to illustrate the importance of notifying your agent. It's crucial that you find the first available moment to call your agent and notify them of these scenarios. Do not wait until you are wrapped and you have gone home, to deal with these issues.

◊ SCENARIO #1 - You are asked to sign a contract which is unfamiliar to you or includes incorrect information about your deal.

Your agent should have prior approval over your contract. With bigger deals, you'll sign a contract prior to showing up on set. In the case of many day player, co-star, and guest star television contracts, you'll receive your contract on set and be asked to sign at that time. If you're unclear what anything means in your contract, or don't know what to look for, then you could be signing a non-agent-approved contract which does not match your deal. By signing, it means you've agreed to those terms. No take-backsies! It's very challenging for us to reverse this after the fact. When in doubt, ALWAYS confirm with your agent that you are signing your proper contract. A quick photo emailed or texted is all it takes.

◊ SCENARIO #2 - You are put in a hazardous situation in a scene.

If you're put in a dangerous situation on set for which you've received no prior knowledge, feel you're at risk of injury, or feel like your life could be in danger, say something immediately. If you don't feel comfortable telling someone on set, sneak away and call your agent. It doesn't matter if another actor feels okay about it, or the pyrotechnics guy says it's perfectly safe. You have a right to voice your concerns if you personally feel unsafe. If you let this go, and don't inform production or your agent, you could risk injury (or worse). And, if you don't speak up, they may assume you do feel safe. Aside from the repercussions of causing you bodily harm, not speaking up can also make it difficult for your agent to argue for additional hazard pay, medical reimbursements, or other remedies after the fact because the producers may not want to claim responsibility. Safety should be a priority on every set and you've got your agent in your corner to help ensure the production is held accountable.

◊ SCENARIO #3 - You are told there is nudity in a scene and are asked to undress

It's a union requirement that if a role requires any form of nudity it must be disclosed in advance, at the time of the offer. The actor must feel comfortable with the extent of any nudity. It's within your power to request to have a conversation with the director so that any sensitivities are addressed prior to closing a deal. Surprises on set that deal with nudity are a huge problem which require immediate notification to your agent. Even if you feel comfortable with having your beautiful, naked, backside revealed, you may be entitled to a bump in pay for such exposure. Your agent will also want to ensure there's a closed set during the shooting of any scenes involving nudity or sexual situations. Your contract should also be supplemented with a Nudity Rider, a consent form that details the specific form of nudity and each scene in which some nudity will occur.

Being on set should be a fun and amazing experience. While unexpected scenarios do arise, keep the communication open with your agent so matters can be dealt with efficiently to ensure your safety and well-being.

8

Share Your Contacts & Connections

I've discussed the importance of networking in this book and I'll reiterate again how careers are often made on great relationships alone. Your agent comes with a set of connections that's constantly growing through ongoing networking and (hopefully) good business practices. But an agent can't know everyone, so what you contribute can create an even bigger network of individuals integral to your career. Your agent can help capitalize on those relationships but, if we don't know about them... well, we don't know about them. So, keep your agent up to speed on anyone you meet or work with whom you've added to your own network. We can use the information in a variety of ways:

◊ Inform a casting director of an existing relationship which could influence you getting in the room

◊ Reach out to your contact directly with your materials so you stay on their radar

◊ Keep track of your contact's projects to seek out work on your behalf.

It's always fun for an agent to have some extra ammunition to get you in the door and often, the connections you've created can be the firepower we need.

Ask, "What Can I Do?" Not, "What's Going On?"

Every time an actor asks me, "What's going on? Is it busy? Do you have anything for me?" I have a knee jerk response: "There's lots going on, I'm always busy, and if I had anything for you, you would be the first to know about it." Of course, I don't say that out loud and this is not the answer they'd be looking for. It's also not the right question.

It's important to realize that, even during the slowest times of the year, there's always "stuff" going on. We are still submitting, pitching, reviewing your materials, troubleshooting our strategy for you, seeking out relationships... I could go on and on. Therefore, we are always busy and always working hard to further your career.

So, the better question to ask is, "Is there anything I can do to help you and help myself create more opportunities?" This presents a pro-active approach to your career, suggests you understand it's a team effort, and indicates you're interested in giving as much as you're receiving. Your agent will be so much more open to this kind of conversation rather than being on the defensive with a barrage of needy-sounding questions.

⑩

Remember My Birthday

Well, not mine specifically (July 6th, thanks for asking), but your own agent's and manager's. Sometimes it's the small things that make a big difference in keeping your relationship with your agent strong. A personal gesture of remembering an important date can make us feel like we aren't just the person sitting at a desk who's supposed to get you auditions, but a human being who, like most everyone, appreciates being acknowledged on a special occasion. It's not about a gift, but the thought. It shows you care and brings a personal element into the equation, which almost always makes someone want to work harder for you.

9 Top 10 Ways To Stay Grounded

> **"**
>
> Don't' be afraid
> to fail. It's not the
> end of the world,
> and in many ways,
> it's the first step
> toward learning
> something and
> getting better at it.
>
> JON HAMM

This is a roller coaster of a business with so many sources of negativity, rejection, and judgment. I cannot stress enough the importance of maintaining a healthy mindset and practicing self-care while pursuing an acting career. It's important to practice strategies to stay grounded, be pro-active, take breaks, and remind yourself why you love what you do.

1

Take A Break From The Biz

It's very easy to get trapped in the bubble of the entertainment world. When you live in a city where it seems every other person is an actor, producer, director, agent… it can feel like there's no escaping. Before you know it, everything outside the bubble is an afterthought. When your world is smaller, the ups and downs feel bigger and it can be hard to feel like you're on solid ground.

Taking a break by getting out of town and surrounding yourself with friends outside the industry will provide perspective and help refresh your outlook on your career. Every time I take a vacation, whether it's a weekend getaway, or a 2-week escape, I always return with renewed motivation. A break from this all-consuming business is healthy for your heart, mind, and spirit, and you'll find it's easier to handle the ups and downs when you have a broader perspective of the world outside.

2

Realize Everyone Peaks At A Different Time

In a competitive business, it's difficult not to compare yourself to others. More times than I can count, I've heard actors say, "My friend is my same type and goes on auditions all the time. Why don't I?" or, "That should be me. We look similar, we play the same type of roles; it doesn't make sense!"

The first thing to understand is that although you might feel you're the same type as someone else, every actor is unique. Your resumé, relationships, personality, work ethic, marketability, mindset, drive, and luck (yes, luck) all contribute to your experience and success as an actor. For some actors, things align much faster, and for others it can take longer. Some actors don't get noticed until they hit a particular age range because, all of a sudden, their type is trending and popping up in all kinds of TV and film projects. Or, as you grow as an actor and develop a better understanding of your type, you'll begin to see more success by focusing on a particular sweet spot. The notion of the overnight success is a myth. 99.9% of actors work hard and pay their dues long before they get their 'big break".

If you stay grounded, dedicated and focused on your goals, it will happen for you exactly when it's supposed to happen. So, if your friend's career seems to be moving at a faster pace than yours, instead of being discouraged or disheartened, be supportive and encouraging. After all, you may actually outpace them some day.

Submit Yourself

Submitting yourself on projects is a great way to feel pro-active and like you're taking charge of your career instead of feeling dependent on your rep or sitting back and waiting for auditions. Actors now have more resources than ever for finding acting opportunities. Actors Access, Casting Networks, and Backstage are three of the primary sites that post jobs which allow actors to submit themselves.

However, you'll want to be choosy with these types of projects. Depending on where you are in your career, some smaller projects may not interest you. Still, be open to the possibility if for no other reason than to keep your auditioning skills sharp. And if you book, you get the opportunity to work. Not every actor can call themselves a "working actor" and when you can, what a sense of validation and accomplishment! Whether you're getting paid in copy, credit and meals, or actual dollars, you'll still feel the reward of being on set, stretching your acting muscle, and collaborating with other artists.

Avoid Access To Casting Breakdowns/Briefs

If you just read number 3 above, you might think I am contradicting my own advice. "Brianna, you just suggested I submit myself on projects, but how am I supposed to do that if I avoid getting breakdowns?"

It helps to explain that there are two points of access for receiving casting breakdowns (or briefs) – Rep Access and Talent Access. The casting sites make available a limited number of project breakdowns to talent, while the more prestigious breakdowns are released only to talent representatives.

As Talent, you should certainly take a pro-active approach and submit yourself on projects. The breakdowns you will have access to are generally smaller projects with lower budgets. However, for new actors, they can be resumé and demo reel builders. Receiving and submitting these breakdowns to keep yourself productive can be a healthy practice and is something I totally encourage.

Breakdowns released only to reps are exclusive for a reason – trust. Casting directors rely on agents to submit wisely: choices based on inside knowledge and needs of a project, professional expertise, and understanding of casting's talent preferences. This trust is developed over time and is at the core of a strong casting director/agent relationship. The more confidence the casting director has that the agent will submit the right actors for a role, the more auditions that agent may receive for their clients.

Access to agent breakdowns is restricted. However, there are some underground sources out there that will provide these breakdowns to actors, usually for a fee. It's not legal, but it happens. It's these agent breakdowns then I encourage you avoid.

Why? One word: sanity. It's very easy to get frustrated when you scan all the projects casting, see all the roles you think you should be auditioning for, and not get called for the opportunity. There are dozens of factors that go into the casting process- many I touch on in this book- so it can be a major head trip to see all these opportunities and not understand why you're not being chosen for them. This feeling can build up over time and lead to frustration, lack of confidence, discouragement and demotivation.

The moral of the story is to trust that your agent or manager is submitting you appropriately and pushing to get you in the room. Your job is to be as fully prepared as possible when that audition call comes in!

Create!

The days of waiting for the phone to ring are over! You must find ways to be pro-active with your career and creating material is one of the best ways. We are living in an exciting time for media and entertainment. Technology, accessibility, and a captive social audience have made the possibilities limitless. The environment is just begging for performers to get out there and CREATE! There are so many stories about how "no-names" have skyrocketed to fame after having taken that first step of creating content. What starts as a smart phone video can turn into a TV show!

Even if your aspirations aren't in filmmaking, look at it as a way to explore new characters on film, collaborate with others, learn what goes into producing and casting, and create material for your demo reel.

I love seeing what my clients create on their own. It inspires me and reminds me of their talent and the new and exciting ways they're taking initiative to help grow their career.

Establish A Support Group Of Actors

It's easy to feel isolated when your chosen profession is Acting. Unless you're on a job going to a set each morning, you don't have an office to go to daily or a team of co-workers sharing a common goal. Your success is often measured only by your individual achievements.

Actors commonly second guess their work and their career choices when faced with prolonged periods of unemployment, scarce auditions or the lack of other types of industry validation. Dealing with these emotions on your own can be difficult and deflating.

The good news? You're not alone. Surrounding yourself with a support system of other actors experiencing the same ups and downs as you will help stave off negative inner dialogue. Being with other actors will remind you that you're part of a community, all riding the same roller coaster. Aside from being an emotional support system for each other, you and your fellow actors can share tips, tricks, info, and resources. Being a positive light for someone else, will feed your own soul, too.

Read Actor Books, Bios & Inspirational Stories

Emily Blunt had a stutter until she was 14 when she was pushed into theater acting. She's now a Golden Globe winning actress. As a teenager, Jim Carrey's family had to live in a van and he bombed his first time doing stand-up. In 1995, he was able to cash a $10,000,000 check he wrote to himself when he first moved to Los Angeles. As a teen and young man, Tyler Perry was abused and bullied and attempted suicide twice. His early productions were flops and he often had to sleep in his car. By 2011, he was named Forbes magazine's highest paid male in entertainment.

Every successful actor has a unique story of their journey to the top.   Learning about other people's experiences is tremendously inspiring. You'll learn that everyone's path is unique just like yours. You'll also find that you're not the only one who feels discouraged at times, has been passed up for a role, deals with emotional rollercoasters, has been close to calling it quits, and gets frustrated with the system. But when you realize that others have gone through the same thing, you'll be more open to learning strategies for managing your emotions, getting over the bumps in the road, and maintaining a healthy mindset. All those behaviors will inevitably lead to a more grounded journey.

Here is a list of some of the top reviewed books from some of the industry's finest:

◊   Bossypants – by Tina Fey

◊   I Can't Make This Up: Life Lessons – Kevin Hart

◊   If Chins Could Kill: Confessions of a B Movie Actor – by Bruce Campbell

◊   King of Comedy: The Life and Art of Jerry Lewis – by Shawn Levy

◊   Not My Father's Son: A Memoir – by Alan Cumming

◊   Five Easy Decades: How Jack Nicholson Became the Biggest Movie Star in Modern Times – by Dennis McDougal

◊   Yes, Please – Amy Poehler

◊   Total Recall: My Unbelievably True Life Story – Arnold Schwarzenegger

◊   My Word Is Bond: A Memoir – by Sir Roger Moore

◊   Lucky Man: A Memoir – Michael J. Fox

◊   Leonard: My Fifty-Year Friendship with a Remarkable Man – by William Shatner

◊ Higher Is Waiting – Tyler Perry

◊ One More Time: A Memoir – Carol Burnett

Have A Hobby Or Other Passion

Enrich your life. It will keep you grounded and make your acting better.

Having laser focus on your career is very important if you want to achieve your goals and dreams. But it's just as important to remember that there's more to life than "Hollywood." Creating a bubble around yourself in which all you do is eat, sleep and breathe acting can result in isolation from the outside world, burnout, and/or depression if you don't get the results you want right away.

Instead, treat your acting career like a regular job. Set some hours where you apply that laser focus, and then discipline yourself to "cut off" from it for a while. Filling your life with other interests and passions will give you a much needed break and help you stay grounded. The benefits are plentiful. Here are a few ideas:

◊ Meet friends, not in the industry, who can provide a change in perspective and a different type of support. Isn't it nice to have friends who aren't constantly going on and on about this audition and that audition, or why so-and-so got the part over me, and all the other conversations that don't serve you? It's refreshing to be with people who are interested in conversations that remind you there's more to life than showbiz.

◊ Experience new adventures, worlds and areas which can serve as inspiration for character development and authenticity in your acting.

◊ Vent. Physical activity is a great way to shake off the frustrations of the showbiz world. Obsessing after an audition is a trap, so instead, do something physical, completely unrelated to acting, that brings you joy and leaves the audition behind. Rock wall? Martial Arts? Sky Diving? Surfing? Camping? Crossfit?

◊ Make money doing something else you love. Most actors have to have a side job when starting out. Go for something you're also passionate about.

9

Set Goals & Work On Them Everyday

There are countless advice books focused on strategies for setting and achieving your goals, so I'm not going to profess to be an expert. I will, however, encourage you to get clear on your goals and commit to taking action towards them as part of your daily work as an actor. By taking charge in this way, you'll set yourself up to experience small victories along your journey, providing invaluable sparks of motivation and accomplishment.

When assessing your goals, a powerful tool is the S.M.A.R.T. goal strategy, a common and effective way to create attainable goals. Start by making a list of your long-term goals. Then, rework them so they fit into the S.M.A.R.T. goal format.

It works like this:

◊ **S. is for SPECIFIC.** Make sure your goals are specific. When a goal is too vague or ambiguous, likely your results will be vague and ambiguous. Your dreams are actually the grand outcome of a series of more specific and precise goals. Consider quality over quantity. Having 3 specific goals instead of 10 lofty and vague goals is a more powerful path to achievement.

1. Example of an "Okay" Goal: *Become a famous TV star.*

2. Example of a "Great" Goal: *Book a series regular role on a sitcom within 5 years.*

The second example is much more specific and provides a clearer benchmark towards the dream of becoming a famous TV star.

◊ **M. is for MEASURABLE.** You should be able to have a measurable indication of when you've achieved your goal. In Example 2, booking a series regular is very measurable; there's no vagueness as to whether you achieved it. Example 1 is too obscure. What is the measure of "famous"? Is it how much money you're making? Is it whether you're in People Magazine? And it's likely different for many people. A measurable goal also means you can assess your progress along the way and enjoy the excitement of moving closer to achieving your goal.

◊ **A. is for ACHIEVABLE.** Your goals should challenge and stretch you but not feel unattainable or too grandiose. You need to feel confident that you can actually achieve them. You'll want to be able to answer questions like: "How will I achieve this goal?" and "Do I possess the skills or do I know where to go to get the skills I need for this goal?".

◊ **R. is for RELEVANT or REALISTIC.** Does your goal make

sense, is it relevant and is it based in reality? Example 1 is already a vague goal, but it's also not even relevant or realistic given how the medium of television has evolved. In today's entertainment industry, when we talk about "what we're watching on TV", we're not only talking about a traditional television series but also big budget digital streaming series on Netflix and Amazon. From an audience perspective, these are all one and the same. Therefore, "becoming a famous TV star" is not only vague but out of touch with the new realities of the entertainment business. Example 2 indicates a sitcom which could live on any of these platforms and fits better within the framework of today's television reality.

◊ **T. is for TIME-BOUND.** Every goal should have a timeframe and projected completion date. You'll notice in Example 2, I enhanced the goal by adding the timeframe of "within five years". Similar to making your goal measurable, if you don't set some time constraints, you won't be able to assess your progress. Deadlines help to keep you motivated. Without them, it's easy to make excuses, procrastinate, and prolong steps towards achieving a goal. Having a target date also means you'll know exactly when to celebrate achieving that goal!

For more detailed information on S.M.A.R.T. goals, including a worksheet, check out:

www.smartsheet.com/blog/essential-guide-writing-smart-goals

Along with implementing the S.M.A.R.T. goal strategy, I think it's incredibly important to break down your goals into micro-goals. Think about all that's needed to achieve your main goal. Using the S.M.A.R.T. goal method, write down all the micro-goals which will lead you toward achievement. Think of them as steps on the staircase towards your main goal. Not only will you feel more in control of reaching your goal, but you'll stay motivated by completing small goals along the way.

Remember Your "WHY"

"You can only become truly accomplished at something you love. Don't make money your goal. Instead pursue the things you love doing, and then do them so well that people can't take their eyes off of you."
-- *Maya Angelou*

The quality of your WHY is proportional to the quality of your WHAT. The stronger your reasons and desire to do something, the more you strive to work hard towards doing that thing and doing it well. Having a clear "why" is CRITICAL to your success. It's like your own personal mission statement that drives you and can be a super powerful motivator.

At some point in your life, you decided to become an actor. Every one of you had a moment when a light went on in your head and heart and you realized, "I need to be an actor." When was the last time you asked yourself, "Why do I love acting?" and "Why did I choose to be an actor?" For some of you, the answers jump right out and are obvious. For others, you may need to remind yourself why you do what you do.

I encourage you to reflect on your "why" and write it down in one powerful statement. Here are some questions and prompts to help you formulate your statement:

◊ "I believe..."

◊ "I am driven by...

◊ "What cause am I working towards?"

◊ "What is the gift I am giving and how will it positively affect others?"

◊ "I would like to improve the lives of others by...."

Congratulations! You now have a powerful mantra that can lead, inform, and inspire your choices throughout your career and life. Write down your Why Statement and post it somewhere where you'll see it on a regular basis. This constant reminder will serve as motivation and encouragement to keep you on track and reignite your fire when you're feeling lack luster.

EXAMPLE: "My desire to become an actor really early on was [that] I wanted to communicate something, to reflect something back to the audience. For me, that was what was powerful. I think that's what's more important than being in the center of the stage. To communicate something" - *Matt Dillon*

Note: Your statement is more powerful if it's based upon feelings, core beliefs, values, passions, and focuses on contribution and impact, instead of personal gains. Furthermore, it is not advised to use making money as part of your why. If you're in it solely to make money then you may lose your passion for the craft. This lack of passion will be evident in your performances and may hold you back.

10 Top 10 Industry Myths

> "
> Hollywood has a way of making everything seem like an overnight success.
>
> KEVIN HART

> Truth is power, so let's set the record straight on some of these industry illusions.

1

You Can Play Anything

Take a headshot of every possible look and think that it will get you more opportunities? Not so much. This may actually work against you by creating more confusion about what type of actor you really are. For example, I would never tell a client who's inherently the bubbly best friend type, to put on an edgy, goth-like outfit and make-up and shoot headshots just so she can look the part in order to get called in on those roles. I would be setting her up for failure in the room.

Yes, it's important to train as an actor in a wide variety of roles. This is how you stretch and grow and discover your strengths and weaknesses. It might also make you feel like you can play any type of character. But when it comes to marketing yourself and targeting roles, remember your Actor Identity and focus on your strengths. Experts excel in one area and being known as a particular type of actor isn't necessarily a bad thing. It gives you the freedom to be the most amazing version of yourself in that niche, thus people will start to take notice and you'll see your career propel forward.

Let me be clear: I'm not saying if you play doctors really well that you should only focus on doctor roles. It's about the character traits you embody and the roles to which these traits best translate. No matter how talented an actor, the reality is that this industry will not accept you in every role, so don't try to be all things to all people!

2

Any Agent Is Better Than No Agent

For the unrepresented actor, it's natural to feel like your number one goal is to get an agent... any agent. I would caution against this. Of course, having an agent is an essential part of your team, but not all agents are created equal. As you might imagine, some may even do more harm than good.

The following are some red flags to look out for when deciding to sign with a particular agent or if it may be time to part ways with your current agent.

◊ Reputation - What is their reputation around town? Have you heard unfavorable stories about the agent? Once is chance, twice is coincidence, and three times is a pattern. If you've heard repeated negative stories, it's more than likely they are true. Your association with such an agent can mean fewer appointments for you. If a casting director doesn't like working with an agent, they may avoid the opportunity by not bringing in their clients. Or if an agent is known for signing every actor that comes their way, that could devalue your talent by association. Don't let someone else's bad reputation bring yours down. year's

◊ Too Many Promises - if there's one thing I've learned about this business, it's that its too unpredictable to make lofty promises. You may meet with an agent who promises to put you on "X" TV show, guarantee you'll make a certain amount of money in a certain amount of time, promise you'll be the next big star in a year's time, promise to get you an audition for the next Star Wars film, or any number of enticing claims.

The reality is that there are just too many variables at play to be able to guarantee auditions or placement in particular projects. Be wary of agents who throw out promises as they are likely just trying to get you to sign and often can't deliver on such promises. This type of agent often comes up short on other aspects of good representation and you'll likely be disappointed in how they guide you and what they offer.

◊ Complacency - An agent who is not submitting you on the right projects or not pitching you is a waste of your time. Dry spells with auditions come and go, but you want to make sure your agent is at least submitting you in a timely manner and pitching you regularly. Unfortunately, there are agents out there who do minimal work and wait to see what appointments come in. They are not actively pursuing opportunities for you beyond just the basic submissions. Months or years can go by without your agent pushing for you, when your career could have otherwise been growing at a faster rate. To put it bluntly, a lazy agent is definitely worse than no agent at all.

So, how do you know if they're just going through the motions? Ask how many times a month they pitch you. Request to see the email pitch they send out. Perhaps they are misrepresenting who you are and haven't updated their pitch with your latest activity and highlights. The last thing you want to do is micro-manage your agent, but it's within your right as their client to question their efforts and hold them accountable if you sense complacency. Be aware that there are many factors not within an agent's control, so focus on the things that are.

In the chapter "Top 10 Tips for Getting an Agent," I point out that when you finally get a meeting with an agent it's also your opportunity to interview them. If you're fortunate to get an offer for representation, consider if the agent is the right fit for you and don't just automatically say yes. In some cases, you'll need to go with your gut.

And lastly, when you do team up with the right agent, don't forget that your work doesn't stop there. Continuing a proactive approach to your career in conjunction with your agent's efforts will see more rapid results and create a much stronger relationship. Everyone wins!

3

Talent Is Everything

I wish. How many times have you seen a major studio film and thought, "Why didn't they hire a better actor for that role?" If the best actor always got the part, then an actor's job would simply be to become the absolute best actor they can be. While it is still true that you need to be constantly training and growing as an actor, it's not everything.

You have to think like a business owner and give energy to all the areas that contribute to growth: networking and relationships, presentation, reputation, marketing and your passion and dedication for what you do. All of these factors, in addition to your acting talent, contribute towards your potential to be hired.

This may be frustrating, but once you understand that you also need to focus on areas besides acting talent, it's empowering. It gives you more ways to take control of the success of your career. It also helps you accept rejection without blaming yourself. Knowing how many factors are at play provides the possibility that they may have loved your performance but you didn't get the part due to variables beyond your control. At the end of the day, remember that even if your talent wins them over, being chosen may come down to a number of factors, sometimes as simple as your height.

It's Not What You Know, It's Who You Know

False, sort of. Sure, relationships play a huge part in the growth of your career. However, it's not only who you know, it's what you do with who you know. Let me be clear, I am not suggesting any compromising or sexual acts. I'm referring to how you nurture and build upon those relationships. Let's say you've met 100 casting directors, but have you kept in touch, marketed yourself smartly, made yourself positively memorable, and authentically built upon the initial introduction? This is just one example. Don't assume that just because you've met someone once or twice that they owe you anything. The value of relationships has been mentioned several times throughout this book. The key is authenticity and creating a relationship built on respect. That's the only way to win fans who are going to support and vouch for you and do so because they choose to, not because they feel manipulated, forced or pressured. But don't forget... you still gotta have the talent to back it up!

You Have To Have A Huge Social Media Following

There are a lot of opinions out there on the importance of an actor's social media and number of followers. I'm here to say that it's important but not the end-all and be-all of becoming a successful working actor.

So, what about the numbers? The number of followers you have on social media certainly carries weight and, in particular situations, may actually tip the scales in your favor. If producers are deciding between two actors, both talented and right for the part, they will start looking at other factors, social media being one of them. Many followers = many eyeballs. A producer stands to gain a valuable marketing opportunity from the actor who has a larger reach on social media. It's important to note that for those with huge numbers of followers, this promotion should not come for free. The number and type of promotional posts should be a negotiating point and can earn you a nice publicity bonus.

Numbers aren't everything, though. In the early 2010's, the rise of the social media influencer naturally caught the attention of Hollywood and there were many attempts to build scripted shows around such influencers. These experiments often resulted in failures because the influencer didn't have the chops to carry a show. The reality is that influencers are often not trained actors and their popularity and content doesn't necessarily translate to scripted programming or movies. I've seen a shift in attitude about the importance of followers for this reason. When it comes to hiring actors for TV and film, it's not enough to just have big numbers. Again, you also gotta have talent.

So yes, your social media presence and online footprint are very important but build your followers smartly and don't worry too much if you don't have hundreds of thousands of followers yet. There are plenty of other reasons to be on social media and it can be a very useful tool in marketing and growing the business that is you. You can read more about the importance of your online brand and presence in the chapter "Top 10 Tech Tools & Tips".

6

The Casting Director Is The One Who Hires You

It might feel like the casting director is the one who hires you – after all, they chose to call you in for the audition, the callback, checked your availability, and came to you with the offer (hopefully!). Casting directors play an essential role in the hiring process but, 99% of the time, they aren't the ones who make the final decision. To win the job, you'll have to get approval from the director, producers and the executives at the network and studio. That's a large number of people that all have to say yes. But you've got to get that very first yes, and indeed that comes from the casting director.

7

Don't Rock The Boat

I can't think of any successful actor who didn't shake things up or take daring action in order to achieve their goals. It's important to understand that you can't please everyone, in this business or any other. Playing it safe will only lead to complacency and, frankly, doesn't make for a very interesting actor. Sometimes you have to make bold choices in order to achieve your desired results. Those choices might make others uncomfortable and they might make you uncomfortable. Author Caroline Myss writes, "Always go with the choice that scares you the most, because that's the one that is going to help you grow." There will always be people who love your work and those who don't care for it, so as long as you aren't harming anyone, take the leap and try rocking that boat!

8

Being A Successful Actor Means I Have To Compromise Who I Am

No job or role is ever so important that you have to say yes if you feel you're sacrificing your own moral code or core beliefs. You'll have to decide for yourself what your personal boundaries are. For some, that might mean no nudity or could mean not accepting an offer from a company whose practices and ethics you oppose. Getting clear on what your limitations are and having conviction in those decisions will make it easier to pass when an opportunity comes along which does not align with your principles. There may be some hard decisions to make.

It's also important to communicate this to your representation so they don't pursue such opportunities. And it goes without saying – but I'll say it anyway – that being asked to engage in sexual conduct in exchange for a role, a job or to please a high-powered individual, is NEVER okay. For additional information about sexual harassment and resources, you can visit my website or go to this webpage:

www.sagaftra.org/files/sa_documents/sag-aftra_code_of_conduct_f2_2_0.pdf

One of the hardest decisions actors can make is to pass on role, especially early in their career. Sometimes an opportunity just seems too great and the benefits seem to outweigh the consequences. But I guarantee: if it doesn't feel right, you'll always feel like you compromised yourself. And the reality is that it's just not necessary. There will always be another opportunity. But there's only one you and you'll want to feel good about your choices and sleep soundly at night.

Actors Are The Most Important Part Of A Productiom

In promoting a movie or TV show, it's the actors that are featured and used to entice the audience to tune in. Thus, actors become the literal and figurative "face" of a production. Perfect fuel for the ego to thrive on. Because of this, it's easy for actors to think that their role is more important than any other member of the crew. This couldn't be further from the truth. What do you think would happen if the boom operator didn't show up? The actor wouldn't be heard. What if the lighting grip wasn't doing their job properly? The actor wouldn't be seen. What if there was no writer? There wouldn't even be any project to begin with. There are so many talented individuals required to create an amazing film or television show, and each performs a unique function essential to that success – from the PA's, Craft Services and drivers, to the editors, stylists, and animal wranglers. The elitist attitude shared by many actors is simply uncalled for and unwarranted. It takes a village.

Following A Formula Will Lead You To Success

There is no one formula for a successful acting career. This book is chock full of tips and tools you can use to help push you towards success. Some will work for you and some won't. What works for one person, doesn't for another. That's how crazy this business is. Persistence, dedication and the passion to try things and be proactive is at the core of it all. You will be continually surprised, underwhelmed, overwhelmed, disappointed, and elated as you journey through your career. **Embrace the ride!**

GLOSSARY OF
INDUSTRY TERMS

A.D. - Assistant Director. Duties may include writing call sheets, setting up shots and directing extras. There are usually multiple A.D.'s on a production, the 1st A.D. being the highest on the assistant directing chain.

Above-the-Line - Refers to the "creatives" whose names and titles actually appear above the line on a production budget. Actors, writers, directors and producers are all considered "above-the-line". All other crew are "below-the-line".

Across-the-Board - Refers to a form of representation when a talent agency represents a client exclusively in all areas, including but not limited to TV, Film, Theatre, Commercials, Print.

Action - Command given by the director to start filming a scene. Often preceded by "rolling", which means the cameras have started to record (roll).

Adjusted Gross Participation - A percentage of the gross receipts less certain costs, such as cost of advertising and post-production.

ADR - Post-production term meaning Automated Digital Recording or Automated Dialogue Replacement. An actor may be called in for an ADR session to re-record dialogue.

Advance - A pre-payment of monies to be counted against any fees due in the future.

AMPAS - Academy of Motion Picture Arts and Sciences.

Apple Box - A box (usually a wooden crate) an actor stands on in order to appear taller for shot.

ASC - American Society of Cinematographers.

Atmosphere - Another term for "background" or "extra" performers.

Avail - An "avail check" is when an actor's availability for a project is checked. To be "on avail" in the commercial industry means the actor's schedule must remain open for the dates of the commercial until further notice. In both instances, an actor's conflicts must be communicated at the time of and for the duration of the "avail" until released or booked.

Back-End Participation - Refers to a deal in which a percentage of a TV or film production's profits is agreed to be paid. Percentages may vary as well as the gross on which the percentage is based.

Back-Nine - A television term referring to an order of nine episodes AFTER both the initial pilot and subsequent 12 episodes are ordered. Together it makes a complete 22 episodes season.

Back-To-One - A direction given to an actor to return to their original position at the beginning of the scene.

Backdoor Pilot - A television pilot filmed as a stand-alone movie so it can be aired regardless of a pilot pick up.

Background - Another term for "atmosphere" or "extra" performers.

BAFTA - British Academy of Film and Television Arts.

Beat - A pause.

Below-the-Line - Refers to crew whose names and titles actually appear below the line on a production budget. Actors, directors, writers, and producers are considered "above-the-line". All other crew are "below-the-line", including but not limited to grips, gaffers, lighting designers, props, wardrobe stylists, make-up artists, and sound engineers.

Best Boy/Best Girl - Right-hand man or woman for the grip in the electrical department on a production.

Billing - On-screen placement and size of an actor or crewmember's credit. Variables include order of credit, whether alone or in a group, and the size of the role.

Biopic - A film based on the real life of a person or biographical material.

Blocking - During rehearsal, "blocking" is an actor's movement throughout the scene as it relates to the overall environment and other actors.

Body Shot - A full length (head to toe) photograph or video of an actor.

Book Out - To inform your representatives of dates in which you are unavailable for auditions and/or work. "Always remember to book out with your agent or manager".

Booking - A confirmed employment opportunity.

Breakdown Services - A web-based service which provides daily posts of project breakdowns which reps use to submit their talent to casting directors.

Broad - An exaggerated and big performance. As in "broad comedy".

Bump - To receive a performance upgrade, particularly in the case of an "extra" who has been given dialogue and is thus "bumped up" to a more favorable contract.

Buyout - A one-time payment which covers all obligations of any future payment and typically covers session/shoot and usage of a commercial, film or TV show. Commonly used for non-union work.

Call Sheet - A daily production document which includes all actors and crew, their respective call times, and scenes to be shot that day.

Call Time - The time you are to report to set.

Camera Left - When looking at the camera, your right.

Camera Right - When looking at the camera, your left.

Cans - Headphones.

Class A - A National Network TV commercial set to air in primetime on a major network which has the greatest potential for high residuals.

Cold Reading - Performing a scene with material not received ahead of time.

Commission - The percentage of a performer's income paid to an agent or manager. Typically, no more than 10% for an agent, and 10-20% for a manager.

Comp Card - A composite of 3-5 photos, usually 5x7, double sided, including a person's measurements. Used primarily for models.

Concept Meeting - A meeting among producers, director and casting directors to discuss the look, feel and tone of each character in the script.

Conflicts (or Commercial Conflicts) - A commercial booking which requires exclusivity from the actor. During the term of exclusivity, the actor cannot book a commercial for another product in the same category (ie: automobiles, fast food restaurants, soft drinks).

Continuity - Making sure that each shot of a scene has the same props, dialogue, extras, wardrobe, make up, etc.

Coogan Law - A California law which mandates that an employer must place 15% of wages earned by a minor in a trust that the minor can only access upon turning legal age.

Copy - Sides (audition scenes) or script.

Coverage (or Script Coverage) - A synopsis of a script which includes the readers thoughts, impressions, and overview of the storyline. It is usually written for busy executives, producers or agents who don't have time to read full scripts themselves and is often used as a screening process.

Craft Service - On-set food and beverage that is available throughout the day, as opposed to catered breakfast, lunch, and/or dinner.

Crew - Apart from the cast, anyone on set who is contributing to the production.

Cut - A director's cue to stop recording.

D.P. - Director of Photography, AKA Cinematographer. Person in charge of setting up, lighting, and making artistic and technical decisions about a how a scene is shot.

Dailies - Raw takes of scenes without any sounds or light adjustment, used to check the action and select the best takes.

Dark Night - An evening in which a theatre has no scheduled performances. (not Batman)

Day-out-of-Days (aka DOOD) - A spreadsheet created by an assistant director with an overview of cast and their respective start date, work dates, hold dates, and finish date.

Dayplayer - A performer hired to work one day at SAG-AFTRA scale.

Deal Memo - A short form agreement outlining the basic terms of a contract.

Deferrment - Payment made at a later date, usually paid out of the revenue of a film. A deferment may not be paid if the film does not see completion or does not generate any revenue.

Demo Reel - A video compilation of select scenes from an actor's performance experience.

Development - The process in which an initial film or TV idea is turned into a finished screenplay. The development period may include optioning the rights to an existing intellectual property (I.P.), commissioning a writer, fine-tuning the script, and creating a treatment.

DGA - Directors Guild of America, the union of film and TV directors, assistant directors and unit production managers.

Drop/Pick-Up - Term used when an actor is "dropped" (or released) from payroll on a project, and then "picked up" at a later date. At least 14 calendar days must transpire between drop and pick up date. This rule can only be exercised once per actor per project.

Dubbing - Recording sound (either music or dialogue) in order to create a track that can be transferred and synchronized to existing film or TV footage. Often used to replace dialogue into another language instead of using sub-titles.

ECU - Extreme close-up.

EPK - Electronic Press Kit aka Press Package. A digital package which includes press clippings, photos, articles, reviews, bio and headshots of an actor, primarily used by a Publicist to promote the actor.

Favored Nations - A term meaning an agreement or understanding that all terms of engagement are equal among all cast members.

Fire in the Hole - Announcement on set: An explosion or gun shot is about to occur.

First Look Deal - A deal in which a studio or network has the first option to produce a filmmaker or writer's project.

First Right of Refusal - If an actor holds the First Right of Refusal this means he/she has the first option among any other actor to accept or refuse a particular role. If a producer holds the First Right of Refusal it means the actor must not enter into any other conflicting contract or project without clearing it with the producer first, at which time the producer can choose to make an official offer or clear the actor for another opportunity.

First-Dollar Gross - The net amount that is a result of the overall gross, less minimal deductions, such as bank fees, taxes and trade dues. The most favorable form of gross participation for the participant. Also referred to as Gross Participation.

Force Majeure - Unforeseeable circumstances, as a result of a greater force beyond one's control, such as a natural disaster, war, union strike, or death. Productions commonly include a Force Majeure clause in their contracts to protect them should production cease due to such an act. Certain contractual obligations can be suspended in these cases.

Forced Call - A requirement that an actor reports to set with less than 12 hours turnaround from the previous days wrap time. Overtime rates/penalties may apply.

Front Office - Refers to the top executives at a company who control the money.

Go-see - A term for an audition or meeting typically used in the model and print world.

Golden Hour (or the Magic Hour) - The period approximately 1 hour after sunrise, or 1 hour before sunset when the natural light is redder and softer, creating incredibly flattering and beautiful camera shots.

Golden Time - Number of hours worked beyond 16 hours. On union productions, each hour pays an additional day rate. Jackpot!

Green Screen - A blank green backdrop in front of which an actor performs so that any desired background can be digitally inserted to give the illusion that the action was really taking place in that environment.

Greenlight - When a studio commits to and gives the go ahead to start pre-production on a project.

Grip - A member of the lighting and electrical team on a set.

Gross Participation - A percentage of the gross receipts of a film or TV production, less minimal deductions, such as bank fees, taxes and trade dues. Also referred to as First-Dollar Gross

Gross Receipts - Total monies from all revenue sources such as box office, rentals, television, licenses, merchandising and ancillary usage.

Helm - To direct a film or TV show. A "helmer" is a term for a director.

HFPA - Hollywood Foreign Press Association. The entity that produces

The Golden Globes.

Hiatus - Period of time when the cast and crew of a television series is on vacation.

Hold - A day when an actor is getting paid but not working. Also, to be "on hold" for a project should require payment for the hold dates vs. an "avail" which does not. The term "hold" is loose and often misused. -The intentions of the "hold" should be clarified.

Holding Area - A designated area for background extras to gather while waiting to shoot.

Honey Wagon - A dressing room trailer with multiple private dressing rooms and one shared bathroom, typically assigned to co-stars and day-players.

Hot Mike - A microphone that is turned on.

Hyphenates - Individuals taking on more than one role, such as Writer-Director, Producer-Director and Actor-Director

IATSE - International Alliance of Theatrical Stage Employees

In Perpetuity - Forever and ever, until the end of time, throughout the universe. Often used in Talent Release's to provide the producer/distributor with unlimited ownership of the work.

In The Can - Film that is ready for broadcast or public viewing.

Ink - To sign a contract.

INT. - A screenwriting term meaning "Interior" in a script.

Key Art - The artwork used on posters and advertisements.

Laugh Track - Recorded audience laughter inserted into a sitcom.

Legit - Term used to describe live theatre & stage productions. Originally used to distinguish between serious theatre and vaudeville/burlesque.

Line Producer - The producer in charge of day-to-day details of a project who keeps things moving forward and on schedule.

Local Hire - Someone who is hired locally and will not receive any travel, hotel, transportation or per diem.

LOI - Letter of Intent/Interest. A letter confirming an individual's intent or interest in participating in a production, pending terms of an official offer. LOI's are often used to "attach" talent in order to attract investors.

Loop Group - A group of people hired to record additional dialogue and background voices for a production.

Looping - The act of recording or re-recording dialogue post-production.

Magic Hour - See Golden Hour.

Mark - The exact position on a set or stage an actor is to stand for a particular shot.

Market - A specific selling region or sales category.

Meal Penalty - A fee paid when a meal is not provided every 6 hours, per the SAG-AFTRA agreement.

Monologue - A lengthy speech performed by an actor without interruption by another actor.

MOS - Means "without sound", coined by a German director who pronounced it "mit out sound".

MOW - Movie of the Week. Originally coined by ABC who would produce TV movies to be aired on a weekly basis. Today, the term is used to describe any made-for-television movie.

MPA/MPAA - Motion Picture Association and Motion Picture Association of America. Representing the interests of studios in America and abroad.

Must Join - The SAG-AFTRA classification for a member who has worked a union job and has used up the 30-day grace period to join the union. According to the SAG-AFTRA agreement, the member must join in order to be hired on his/her next union job.

Net Profit - Revenue remaining after all allowable deductions.

Notes - Feedback on an actor's blocking or performance, given after a rehearsal, by the director, musical director, choreographer or stage manager.

Off-Book - An actor's performance when they have their scenes fully memorized and don't need to rely on the sides or the script.

On Location - A film set, other than a studio lot, where filming takes place.

On or About - A work date with the flexibility of shifting 1 day before or after, without producer repercussions.

On The Bubble - A TV show that has an unclear fate and "could go either way" – get cancelled or renewed.

On-Camera - Term that has become known to mean "Commercial" work. On-Camera representation refers to a Commercial Agent.

Open Call - An audition open to the public.

Option (actor) - Producer's right to employ, or continue employment of an actor, typically built into series regular TV contracts, and multi-picture deals. Options are typically consecutive and in 1 year increments.

Option (property) - A producer's acquisition, from a seller, of the rights of a property (book, story, etc.) that guarantees no one else can acquire these rights nor produce a work based on the property. Options usually cover a certain period of time.

Out Takes - Originally filmed clips which do not make the final edit of a project. Often referred to as 'bloopers'.

P.A. - Production assistant. Usually in charge of managing the extras and fulfilling a variety of production tasks.

P.O.V. - "Point of View" – the perspective from which a scene is filmed –from the hero's POV, a secondary character or any other actor's POV.

Package/Packaging - During the development phase, packaging is when a talent agency attaches a team of creative people (ie: writer, director, actors), all of whom they represent, to a project. The agency receives a packaging fee from the producers in lieu of client commission.

Payola - A secret payment or bribe to a producer or decision maker to persuade a particular outcome.

Per diem - Translates to "for each day". The daily meal allowance provided to talent while on location.

Percenter - An agent. Refers to the 10% commission they receive. Also known as a Ten-percenter.

Period - A project described as a "period piece" is one that takes place in a past time period or era.

PGA - Producers Guild of America.

Photo Double - An actor used to stand in for a principal actor who is unavailable or only seen partially. A Photo Double does not have any speaking lines.

Pick-Up - The notification when a studio or network elects to order a pilot or a series.

Pilot - The first episode written for a series. A pilot is used to determine whether a network or studio will order the full series.

Pilot Presentation - A smaller production of a pilot to give a network or studio a feel for a series in hopes of getting a greenlight to produce a full scale pilot.

Pitch/Pitching - The act of selling your idea, script, or talent. Convincing someone to invest in your idea or hire your talent for their project.

Playbill - The show program for a play which includes actor and crew bios.

Plug - To promote an upcoming project.

Plus 10 - The 10% agency commission negotiated by an agent in addition to the talent's base fee.

Points - A percentage of the profits for a film or TV property provided to the talent or creatives as part of their compensation package.

Post or Post-Production - The work, after principal photography, that involves editing, special effects, music, sound mixing, etc.

Pre-Read - An acting audition that is typically not recorded and used to familiarize the casting director with an unknown actor. Occurs prior to a callback or producer's session.

Pre-Sale - Sales of a film or TV show to a particular territory prior to completion and usually arranged to raise funds for the production.

Principal - An actor with lines, paid at least union scale.

Pro-Rata - Fees which are a proportion of a larger fee. Commonly used to calculate hourly rates based on a day rate, or daily rates based on a weekly rate.

Protection - An additional film take as 'protection' that the director got what she needed. Also known as 'insurance'.

Publicist - A person hired to create public awareness and promote another person or project.

Put Pilot - A deal to produce a pilot that includes substantial penalties if the pilot is not aired. Under this type of deal, the likelihood of a pick-up is almost guaranteed.

Reader - A person hired to read opposite auditioning actors in a casting session.

Recall - At the end of an actor's filming day, they are asked to return (or 'recalled") for an additional day of services.

Release (or Talent Release) - Usually refers to talent allowing the producer to use his or her likeness on film and soundtrack and "releasing" the producer of any liability.

Residuals - Royalties paid for the use and continued screenings of a property, most commonly used for commercials, television broadcasts and various types of film distribution.

Rider - An addendum to a contract which outlines additional and special terms of employment.

Right-to-Work - A "Right to Work" state (ie, Georgia, Florida, Nevada) is one in which an individual is not required to join a union to work.

Rolling - A term meaning the cameras are on and recording.

Run - The length of time a film appears in a theatre, or the length of time and territory in which a commercial is anticipated to air.

SAG-AFTRA - The professional actor's union that lobbies and organizes on behalf of actor employment rights. To become a SAG-AFTRA actor, you have to pay the initiation fees and annual dues to maintain your membership. As a member, you are able to take advantage of the services of the union and be hired on union productions.

SAG-AFTRA Eligible - An actor who has earned eligibility to join SAG-AFTRA by being cast in a principal role, being a member of an affiliated union or has earned 3 vouchers from doing union extra work.

Scale - The minimum daily or weekly fee that an actor must be paid, according to SAG-AFTRA.

Screen Test - A filmed audition to determine if an actor is suitable for a particular project. A screen test is usually performed in front of executive level decision makers at a network or studio.

Session Fee - Payment for an actor's services for filming one day on a commercial.

Short Order - In television, a network order of less than 13 episodes.

Showrunner - A leading or executive producer responsible for the day-to-day operations of shooting a TV show who holds ultimate authority over creative and management decisions.

Sides - Scenes from a script that are selected for auditioning purposes. The term originated from a time when an actor would only receive their lines, plus a cue, hence only their "side" of the story.

Signatory - A company that has signed an agreement with the union (SAG-AFTRA, DGA, etc) agreeing to abide by the union production rules.

Slate (actor) - In an audition, an actor states, on camera, her name, representation and often height prior to performing the scene(s).

Slate (scene) - While filming, an audible declaration of the scene and take number about to commence.

Sleeper - A film or TV show with limited advertising and hype which becomes a surprise hit... usually thanks to word of mouth or critical acclaim.

Spec - Short for 'speculative'. Refers to an un-commissioned script, written on the chance that a producer will pay you for it later,

Spot - A television or radio commercial.

Stand-In - An actor used in place of a principal actor to rehearse their blocking and stage direction so the cameraman, lighting designer, and other set crew can make adjustments prior to actual filming.

Station 12 - A report provided by SAG-AFTRA which informs casting and producers of an actor's employment status.

Stills - Still photographs taken on set during filming. Also called Photo Stills or Film Stills.

Storyboard - Frame by frame thumbnail size drawings of scenes, with dialogue cues, to indicate camera shots and angles.

Strip Show - A TV show which is intended to air 5-6 days per week and is often in syndication.

Studio - A production and distribution company which owns the facilities to produce and film movies and television, and who lease their property to networks and production companies for filming. Studios are parent companies of several other production entities.

Studio (Major) - The following 5 studios are considered the "Majors" : Disney, Paramount, Universal, Columbia Pictures & Warner Brothers.

Studio (Mini-Major) - The "Mini-Majors" are the large production companies which compete among the Majors, such as Lionsgate, Amblin, & MGM.

Studio Zone - Per SAG-AFTRA, it's the 30-mile radius from the intersection of West Beverly Blvd and North La Cienega Blvd in Los Angeles. In New York City, it's the 8-mile radius starting at Columbus Circle. A production can film anywhere within this zone without having to pay cast & crew for travel and accommodations.

Stunt Bump - Additional pay to compensate for performing hazardous or dangerous scenes.

SVOD - Subscriber-video-on-demand. Programming which is only available on a paid subscription platform (Netflix, Hulu Plus, YouTube Premium, etc.) and which allows the user to watch programs at any time of their choosing.

Syndication - Distribution of a TV series to a cable, regional, or inde-

148

pendent distribution channel.

Table Read (aka 'Read Through') - The director and actors sit around a table and read through the script to familiarize themselves with the project and fellow cast members.

Taft-Hartley - A law that allows non-union actors to work one union job before having to join a union.

Take - Each attempt at filming a scene with the goal of achieving the desired performance.

Tent-Pole - A studio feature film expected to be their biggest money-maker for any given season.

Test Audience - A special screening before an audience to measure the success of a project by receiving feedback about which scenes should stay or go.

Test Deal - A deal in which an actor shoots scenes of a pilot in front of producers, network and studio executives to determine final casting choices. All terms of the potential actor's employment on the series are negotiated within the Test Deal.

Topline - To receive top billing, above the titles, in a film or TV show.

Trades - The various entertainment industry trade publications which include Daily Variety, Hollywood Reporter, Deadline Hollywood, et. al.

Trailer (on set) - The mobile dressing room assigned to an actor. Size may vary and is often a negotiating point in talent deals.

Trailer (of a show) - A two-minute preview synopsis of a film or TV show to entice a potential audience.

Treatment - A short (1-6 page) synopsis of a script which includes a plot outline and character descriptions.

Turnaround (status) - A script in "turnaround" has ceased development by a studio and is available to be shopped around.

Turnaround (time) - Period of time between cast & crew wrap time and call time the following workday. Union rules require a 12-hour minimum turnaround or penalties accrue.

Two-Shot - Camera shot with two people in the frame, usually shot from the waist up.

Type Casting - Casting performers based solely on physical appearance or personality.

Under Five (U/5) - A role classified as having 5 lines or less, which has its own contract and pay rate. This category of role is only applicable to AFTRA legacy shows (shows operating under the AFTRA contract prior to the SAG-AFTRA merger)

Understudy - An actor hired to learn the role of another actor and be on call should the regular actor be unavailable or ill.

Upfronts - Presentations held by the TV networks to showcase their programming slates for the coming season. These are attended by advertisers and the media for the purpose of selling commercial airtime in advance. The Upfronts have typically taken place annually during the third week in May, in New York City. However, new digital and cable platforms have influenced the schedule and certain distributors present their Upfront as early as March.

Upgrade - A rate increase from a smaller role to a larger one, typically from "extra" to "principal". In commercials, an upgrade can be from a group contract to a principal.

UPM - Unit Production Manager. On a film or TV show, the person hired by the producer to oversee the budget, scheduling, locations, and hiring of below-the-line crew.

Usage Fee - Payment due to an actor for a particular use of footage that contains their performance or image. Term is typically used in the commercial industry where residuals are based on commercial usage in specific territories or markets.

VOD - Video-on-demand. Any programming on a platform which allows the user to to watch a program at the time of their choosing. May include free, pay-per-view, or subscription based content.

Voice-Over - An off-camera, audio performance to produce audio tracks most often mixed over music and sound effects.

Vouchers - A document given to "extra" performers for each day of work to be submitted to receive payment.

Walk-Away Meal - In lieu of a prepared meal on set, the producers may call for a 1-hour period of time to allow cast and crew to "walk away" from set and get a meal in a nearby area. If it's a SAG-AFTRA production, per diem for that meal must be paid.

Walk-On - A non-speaking role for an "extra" performer who will appear on-camera.

Weather Day (Rain Day) - An extra shoot day planned in case inclement weather postpones a regularly scheduled shoot day.

Weekly Player - A performer hired to work a minimum of 1 week on a SAG-AFTRA production.

WGA - Writers Guild of America.

Wild Spot - Use of a television commercial in individual markets and cities rather than on national network television.

Work-for-Hire - Under the Copyright Act this is either 1) work completed by an employee within the scope of their employment; or 2) a specially commissioned work (e.g. a motion picture, a contribution to a collective work) to which all parties expressly agree (and sign on to) before work begins.

Workprint - A picture or sound-track print, usually a positive, intended for use in editing to prevent the original from exposure to any wear and tear until the final cut.

Wrap - A word used to acknowledge that the scene being shot (or the work of the day) is complete. "It's a Wrap!"

Zed Card - See Comp Card.

www.tentoptensbook.com

CPSIA information can be obtained
at www.ICGtesting.com
Printed in the USA
LVHW110338030221
678219LV00006B/465